REDHILL, REIGATE &

FAMILY HISTORY GUIDE

TO LOCAL RECORDS

A guide for those interested in researching local and family history, with examples of the main records available to the public. Although the content of this book refers to Reigate and adjacent Parishes, in principle similar records are available in other county record offices, libraries and the Public Record Office

Arthur Hawkes & Jackie Johnson

REDHILL CENTRE
FOR
Local & Family History

ISBN 0-9537532-3-9

© Copyright Redhill Centre for Local and Family History 2000
All rights reserved.

Although every attempt has been made to check the information contained in this book, the Publishers are not responsible for its content or accuracy.

printed by
RAYMENT PRINTERS
5 Horsham Road Dorking, Surrey

Published by: Redhill Centre for Local & Family History
Redhill Library, Warwick Quadrant
Redhill, Surrey, RH1 1NN
Tel. no. 01737 773204 Fax no. 01737 778020
e-mail: redhill.centre@surreycc.gov.uk
http://www.surreyweb.org.uk/redhill-history-centre

Acknowledgement

We are extremely grateful for all the kind support, encouragement, guidance and facilities provided by Redhill Library staff, and the Surrey History Service staff at Woking and in particular to Sally Jenkinson, Janet Nixon and David Robinson who kindly reviewed the book in detail and provided expert advice on the content and copyright compliance.

A debt of gratitude is also owed to the Holmesdale Museum and in particular to Mary Slade, Secretary for searching out specific documents and illustrations from their collections, which have been incorporated in this book.

Marion Brackpool, President of the Reigate & District Family History Group also provided invaluable help in vetting the content of the book and provided helpful guidance for which we are very appreciative.

The publication of this book would not have been able to proceed without the financial support provided by the Heritage Lottery Fund and the kind donations made by those individuals and organisations listed on the back page for which we are very grateful.

The following Illustrations are reproduced by permission of the Surrey History Service at Woking:

Page	Description	Reference
21	Electoral Register Reigate 1875	(SHC QS6/7A/90)
23	Buckland Baptism 1759/60	(SHC 2998/1/1)
24	Merstham Marriage 1808	(SHC P23/1/8)
25	Redhill Baptism 1880	(SHC P49/200/1/2)
26	Buckland Marriage 1863	(SHC 2998/1/)
73	Nutfield Court Baron 1738	(SHC 67/1/8)
74	Reigate Manor Survey 1663	(SHC 371/2/8/3/7A)
75	Reigate Manor Rents 1700	(SHC 371/2/8/3/7)

Page	Description	Reference
37	Gatton Church 1809 from "The Parish Registers of Gatton Co Surrey by Bannerman	*(SHC Library)*
54	Reigate Free School 1822	*(SHC 4348/2/43/2)*

The following illustrations are reproduced with permission of the organisations or Individuals noted next to each item:

11	Marriage certificate	*(Public Record Office 2A 1351)*
13	Birth certificate	*(Public Record Office 2A 168)*
14	Death certificate	*(Public Record Office 2A 137)*
17	1841 Census Return	*(Public Record Office HO107/1076/14)*
18	1851 Census Return	*(Public Record Office HO107/1599/1)*
39	Nutfield St Peter & St Paul	*(Copyright Arthur Hawkes)*
40	Redhill St Johns	*(Copyright Arthur Hawkes)*
42	Reigate St Mary Magdalene	*(Copyright Arthur Hawkes)*
52	Redhill Frenches Road School	*(Copyright Arthur Hawkes)*

56   Reigate National Infants School 1854 from the Illustrated London News dated 16th of Decenber 1854. *Reproduced by permission of the British Library*

59   International Genealogical Index page: Reproduced by permission of the Family History Library of the Church of Jesus Christ of Latter-Day Saints.

Cover picture: by permission of (Art Archive/Bradford City Art Gallery/Eileen Tweedy). Painting by the British Artist James Charles 1851-1906. Signing the Register.

Contents

Chapter	Title
1	Introduction and brief history of Locality
2	Civil Registers
3	Census & Electoral Records
4	Church of England Parish Registers
5	Non-conformist and Roman Catholic Records
6	Churches, Cemeteries and Graveyards
7	School Records
8	International Genealogical Index
9	Wills and Administrations
10	Taxation Records
11	Newspapers, Periodicals & Directories
12	Earlier Genealogical Sources
13	Local Genealogical & Historical Material

Select Bibliography

Useful Addresses

Index

ILLUSTRATIONS

Reigate and District Parish Map sketch	2
Time Line Records 1714 - 1952	8
Time Line Records 1509 - 1714	9
Granny & Grandson sketch	10
Marriage Certificate	11
Birth Certificate	13
Death Certificate	14
Civil Register Review form	15
Example of 1841 enumerator's return	17
Example of 1851 enumerator's return	18
Location of Census Records for Reigate & District	19
Example Part of Reigate Foreign 1875 electoral register	21
Extract from 1759/60 Buckland Baptism Register	23
Marriage registration standard format from 1774	24
Baptism & Burial registration from 1812	25
Post 1837 Marriage Register	26
Copies of local Parish Registers held at Redhill Library	27

Betchworth parish records	34
Buckland parish records	35
Bletchingley & Gatton parish records	36
Gatton- St Andrews Church	37
Leigh & Merstham parish records	38
Nutfield St Peter & St Paul Church & parish records	39
Redhill St John's parish church	40
Redhill St John's Church parish records	41
Redhill St Matthew's parish records	41
Reigate Parish Church - St Mary Magdalene	42
Reigate St Mary's parish records	43
Frenches Road School	52
Reigate Free School 1822	54
Reigate National School - London Road	56
IGI Extract	59
Extract Nutfield Court Baron	73
Manorial Court Survey Reigate	74
Manorial Rental Record Reigate	75

Chapter One

Introduction

Fascination with the past through the pursuit of genealogy and local history study was once the hobby of the rich, as is evidenced by the many documented pedigrees held by the landed gentry or published in early books. However as the working and middle classes have become more affluent through succeeding generations, interest in tracing back one's ancestors has become very popular with people of all ages and backgrounds.

Through the latter half of the 20th century interest in genealogy and local history study has accelerated at an unprecedented rate, mainly by increased awareness of the processes involved, through training courses and the many excellent books now available on this subject. Younger people are being encouraged to take a greater interest in local history through practical projects at school.

In Surrey in recent years family and local history groups have been encouraged by the county record offices and the library service to set up centres in their local libraries which are more readily accessible by the local population. These centres are supported by the library service through the provision of space, equipment and resources such as microfiche, film or hard copy records and are managed and maintained by volunteers from the local history groups. Centres within the east Surrey area include Redhill, Horley and North Tandridge, others will no doubt be established in future years.

The establishment of the Redhill Centre for Local & Family History has proved to be very popular with local people of all ages since its inception in 1996. Interests range from searching out genealogical records in order initially, to draw up the family tree, local research for history projects by pupils from schools, or private research into specific areas of local history interest in order to prepare a publication or article. Whatever the subject the many questions asked of the volunteers who maintain the centre have shown that there is a need for a simple guide to the many records held either by the centre or at other locations and also how they should be used to access the information being sought. This guide is therefore an attempt to meet this need and it should be particularly valuable to individuals new to the subject as well as a useful source reference for the more experienced genealogist.

The records most commonly used by genealogists and local historians are outlined in the various chapters and may apply to other counties. The prime objective of this guide however is to identify the location of those records specific to East Surrey, and in particular the parishes of St Mary's Magdalene Reigate, St Mathew's Redhill, St John's Earlswood, St Emanuel Sidlow, St Luke South Park, St Bartholomew's Leigh, St Michael's Betchworth, St Mary Buckland, St Andrew Gatton St Katherine's Merstham, St Peter & St Paul Nutfield and St Mary's Bletchingley. Some of the records will of course include adjacent parishes, so if in doubt it is always worth checking out specific records to ascertain their actual coverage.

Reigate and District Parish Map

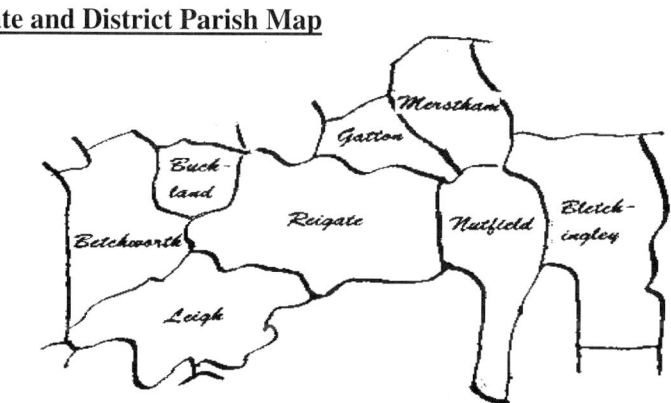

A little History
The history of Reigate and its surrounding districts has been documented in some detail by a number of well known historians including: Wilfred Hooper's *Reigate its story through the ages*, Palgrave's *Illustrated handbook to Reigate 1860*, Manning & Bray's *History of Surrey*, Aubrey's *History of Surrey* and Taylor's *Reigate the adventures of a Surrey town*, to name but a few.

Taylor does in fact summarise the key events that have taken place in Reigate's history, The most significant of which are noted in outline form below.

Initially, he highlights the importance of the old road, later known as Pilgrim's Way to the development of the town and its history. Long before the pilgrims the North Downs had been chosen as the most suitable route for the great road between the west and east of England, to the south lay impenetrable forest and to the north the marshy Thames valley. In the reign of Henry III Winchester held greater importance than London. To reach Canterbury from Winchester the main road lay along the ridge past Guildford and Reigate.

When William the Conqueror won the battle of Hastings in 1066 it is claimed that he sent his army along Pilgrim's Way to hold the roads from Winchester and Chichester. He later came to Dorking to rejoin his forces. He recognised its strategic value and remembered it when he came to reward his followers with lands. It was to gain these that the Barons had followed William to England. The man most favoured in Surrey at that time was Richard de Tonebridge. To strengthen his position Richard built a castle at Bletchingley. Reigate remained in the hands of Edith, widow of Edward the Confessor who had bequeathed it to her. She held it to her death in 1075. The manor then passed to the King William the Conqueror.

In 1087 William de Warenne was created Earl of Surrey and was given the Manors of Reigate, Dorking, Shere, Vachery and Fetcham by the Crown.

Soon after being created Earl, the first Earl of Surrey died and was succeeded by his son, also William. It is believed he built himself a castle at Reigate. This gave the King control over the great road between Canterbury and Winchester and also enabled William to keep a close watch on the De Clares at Bletchingley whose loyalty to the King had begun to wane.

William de Warenne, 2nd Earl of Surrey, married Isabel, daughter of the Count of Vermandois. It was her family's coat of arms, gold and blue chequers, which the de Warennes adopted as their own. He died in 1138 and was succeeded by his son, yet another William, who held the title until his death in 1149. His only child, Isabel, succeeded to his vast possessions. William of Blois, her first husband was the second son of King Stephen. He died in 1159 and his widow took a third husband, Hamelin of Anjou, half brother of Henry II. Her son the sixth Earl had a difficult part to play. Louis of France came over in 1216 to fight with John for the crown. Reigate castle came into Louis's possession, probably without fighting because de Warenne had decided to join the French. Louis passed on triumphantly to Guildford but was then recalled to France on urgent business. The sixth Earl thought it wise to change sides again and support the young King. At his death in 1240 he was followed by his infant son, John, who is remembered as the hero of the rusty sword incident. In 1279 his title to the lands he held was questioned. It was said he flourished "an ancient rusty sword" crying, "here is my warranty, my ancestors came over with William the Bastard and conquered their lands with the sword, and with the sword will I defend them against any who wish to seize them". This was eventually resolved at Guildford Court. One of the Judges at this trial was named John de Reygate.

At the battle of Lewes, 1264, Warenne fought for the King. Reigate was again filled with soldiers on their way with Simon de Montfort to attack the King. The King was defeated. The de Warennes escaped and fled to France to await events while de Montfort took possession of Reigate

Castle. In 1265 the exiles returned and fought at the battle of Evesham where de Montfort was killed and De Warenne recovered his Manor. The last of the de Warennes died in 1347. The estate passed to his brother in law Edmund, Earl of Arundel. Richard Fitzalan grandson of Edmund was beheaded for treason in 1397 after being lured from Reigate Castle. Reigate passed to Arundel's son in law, Thomas Mowbray, Earl of Nottingham but in 1398 he was banished because of a feud with the Duke of Hereford. Reigate was then granted to John Holland, Duke of Exeter, the King's half brother, who was beheaded in 1400 for conspiring against the King, Henry IV, who then restored Arundel's son Thomas to his father's estates. On the Earl's death without issue in 1415 the estate passed to his three sisters, Elizabeth, Joan and Margret. The division and descent of the manor of Reigate from then on is somewhat confused as is illustrated by Manning and Bray's *History of Surrey, Volume 1, Page 282.*

The middle ages saw the development of the church with its priests. In those days great men who were not soldiers usually became Churchmen. Reigate became the resting place of the devout when they travelled to Canterbury to worship before the shrine of St Thomas Becket. They entered Reigate via Colley Hill along a path which took them through Nutley Lane to reach the west end of the High Street. The Red Cross Inn, still standing but now renamed Tap and Spile, dealt with travellers for almost 500 years. The Market House in the centre of the High Street was formally a chapel dedicated to St Thomas Becket. The only remaining chapel is the one dedicated to St Lawrence located next to what was the old Whitehart Hotel. The foundation of Reigate Priory was probably laid in the reign of Henry III but was completed in 1298.

Tudors and the reformation brought a striking change. The Lords of Reigate were no longer great barons but obedient subjects and servant of the crown. A survey in James I reign describes Reigate castle as greatly decayed with a very small house.

At the time of the threat of invasion by the Spanish in 1588 Reigate was ordered to find 836 men to meet the enemy; watches were posted along the hills to fire beacons when the invasion began, but they were never lit as the Armada was defeated at sea under the command of William Howard.

Besides the Howards there were other great families holding lands in Reigate. In 1627 Lord Monson who supported the Roundhead cause purchased various shares of land holding in Reigate. Surrey was not much disturbed by the Civil War. However the county folk around Reigate on the whole were loyal to the King. Several hundred gathered at Dorking in 1648 to draw up a petition calling for a change in the government and a return of the King was presented at Westminster. This was rejected and Parliament sent a regiment of soldiers to put down the revolt. Many were killed or wounded. Almost the last revolt against Cromwell's Government was planned to begin just outside Reigate in 1659. It was again Audeley who was sent to suppress it. Lord Monson sat in judgement at the trial of Charles I. The estates at Reigate were given to Charles II's brother, James, Duke of York. But kingship was not a stable trade in those days, and before many years had passed James himself was sailing over the seas, and William III took the crown. In the year 1697 the manor was granted by William to John, Lord Somers, the great Lord Chancellor; and his family or its branches remained in the town until the early 1900's.

Since the Reformation Reigate settled down into a quite trading town. The market place was moved from the west end of the High Street, where it lay before the Red Cross Inn, to the east end. The emphasis changed from a religious shrine with three chapels into a trading place.

In 1840 with the building of the railways Redhill town developed as a sub district to Reigate and was known as Warwick Town. The Railway provided the opportunity for people to move into the country yet still travel to work in the City of London. In 1867 bribery was rife in politics and Reigate was disfranchised for corrupt members of Parliament. The Reform Act of 1867 brought voting rights to all male house owners residing in the Borough for at least one year and all male lodgers paying at least £10 per annum in rent and residing for one year. Only 70% of male householders qualified for inclusion in the electoral roll. 15% of all householders were excluded because they were women.

Records

Documented records are the life-blood of genealogy, without which it would be impossible to trace back the key events that took place in the lives of our ancestors. Many records have been generated though the ages as a result of Manorial or Governmental administration and control imposed on the population. As far as tracing back ones own family, to get back to the late 1600s would be a significant achievement. A few genealogists have managed to uncover documents that have enabled them to trace their family line back further, but this is generally limited to the nobility who have kept records through many generations. Unfortunately many documents that were in use more than two hundred years ago have either been destroyed or deteriorated to such an extent that they are difficult if not impossible to read.

The records of greatest value to the genealogist are depicted graphically in the following chart, which identifies the approximate period and reign that they were in use. Those records which will be of interest to the beginner includes, Civil Registers, the International Genealogy Index (IGI), The Census, Street Directories, Electoral Registers and Newspapers. These will be discussed in greater detail under specific chapters.

The reason for not showing census records earlier that 1841 is that they are of little use to the genealogist as explained in the relevant chapter.

Timeline 1952- 1714

	House of Windsor						House of Hanover					
	Elizabeth II	George VI	Edward VIII	George V	Edward VII	Victoria	William IV	George IV	George III	George II	George I
	19 52	19 36		19 36	19 10	1 901	18 37	18 30	18 20	17 60	17 27	1714
Civil Registers	1837 to Now											
Directories	1860 to 1950											
Census (FH Interest)	1841 1851 1861 1871 1881 1891											
Electoral Registers	1832 to Now											
Parish Registers	1558 to Now											
Non-Conformists	1660 to 1837											
School Records	1879 to Now											
Death/Estate Duty	1796 to 1903											
Wills	1828											
Petty Sessions												
Pallots Marriage Index	1790 to 1812											
Land Tax	1772 to 1832											
Military Records	1757 to 1876											
Local Newspapers	1854 to Now											
Gentlemans Magazine	1731 to 1868											
Apprentices	1563 to 1814											
Settlement Certificates	1662 to 1876											
Window Tax	1696 to 1851											
Poll Books	1696 to 1872											
Feet of Fines	? to 1834											
Hearth Tax	1664 to 1689											
Poor Law Records	1601 to 1834											
& Board of Guardians												
Lay Subsidy	1542 to 1545											
Manorial Documents	1066 to 1925											
Maps,Surveys, Terriers												
Surrey Taxation returns												
Quarter Sessions	1388 to 1888											

Timeline 1714-1509

	Stuart									Tudor				
	Ann	William III	James II	Charles II	Cromwell			Charles I	James I	Elizabeth I	Mary I	Edward VI	Henry VIII	
	1714	1702	1688	1685	1660	1659	1653	1649	1625	1603	1558	1553	1547	1509
Civil Registers														
Directories														
Census														
Electoral Registers														
Parish Registers														
Non-Conformists														
School Records														
Death/Estate Duty														
Wills														
Petty Sessions														
Pallots Marriage Index														
Land Tax														
Military Records														
Local Newspapers														
Gentlemans Magazine														
Apprentices														
Settlement Certificates														
Window Tax														
Poll Books														
Feet of Fines														
Hearth Tax														
Poor Law Records														
Elizabethan Lay subsidy														
Lay Subsidy														
Manorial Documents														
Maps, Surveys, Terriers														
Surrey Taxation returns														
Quarter Sessions														

Chapter Two

Civil Registers

Civil Registers are one of the first set of records to search when tracing your family history working backwards from yourself through your parents and grandparents. Initially establishing and drawing up the first part of the family tree by discovering the dates of the most important events in their lives of your family, namely their births, marriages and deaths and adding other key information as it is discovered. Any information not supported by certificates will need to be checked for accuracy. The memories of older members of the family are not always reliable.

Before starting down this road you are strongly advised to talk to all the living members of your family including aunts, uncles and cousins to establish if anyone has already carried out some family history research and to obtain copies of any relevant documentation they have including birth, marriage & death certificates. There is no point in re-inventing the wheel particularly as such research is time consuming and does involve some expenditure.

Civil Registration in England and Wales started on the 1st of July 1837 following the Birth and Death Act and the Marriage Act of 1836 which imposed a legal requirement for all births, marriages and deaths to be registered. The general public has the right of access to the indexes of these records. Microfilm copies of the indexes are available at a number of County Record Offices, the PRO at Kew and also at a number of Mormon Church family history centres. The indexes provide a name and reference number plus the maiden name of the mother for births after July 1911, the spouse's surname after 1912 for marriages and the age of death after 1866 for deaths. Copies of the certificates, which provide all the valuable genealogical information can only be obtained (for a fee) from the Family Record Centre in London or the Registration Office in the Registration district where the event took place. Always start from known facts and work backwards in time towards discovering the unknown step by step.

On the assumption that you start with your parents, marriage certificate the following information is typical of that provided by this document and clearly provides a link to and identifies the names of the Grandparents and their professions:

| Date of Marriage | Name & Surname | Age | Previous Condition | Rank or Profession | Residence at time of marriage | Fathers name & Surname | Rank or Profession of Father |

Registration District — Church & Parish — County

Copyright of Public Record Office

Either the male or the female line could be traced back as preferred. Assuming however the male line is chosen then the next step would be to obtain the birth certificate of your father. If this cannot be obtained from him or your relations then you will need to look up the birth indexes at any of the locations previously noted but preferably at the Family Record Centre in London as the certificate can be ordered as soon as you have located the reference number from the index. As noted above, his birth date can be generally calculated from the age given on the marriage certificate previously discussed. Use this as a starting point to look up the indexes. It may be necessary to look up several years either side of this date as the age given on the marriage certificate was not always accurate or the registration did not always take place in the same quarter as the birth.

At the Family Record Centre you look up the indexes in hard copy quarterly manuals arranged alphabetically by surname. Disabled people can look up the indexes on microfiche. The books are quite heavy to handle but quicker to use. The books are clearly identified by colour. Red for births, Green for marriages and black for deaths. All entries give the registration district of the event, not the village or town where it occurred.

When you find the correct entry take a note of the **Registration District**, the **Volume Number** and the **Page Number** as this will be required to be entered on the certificate application form.

Once the application form has been completed hand it in at the counter together with the required fee. You will need to note whether it is to be posted to you or collected. It takes typically four working days to process.

Example: Birth Certificate information provided

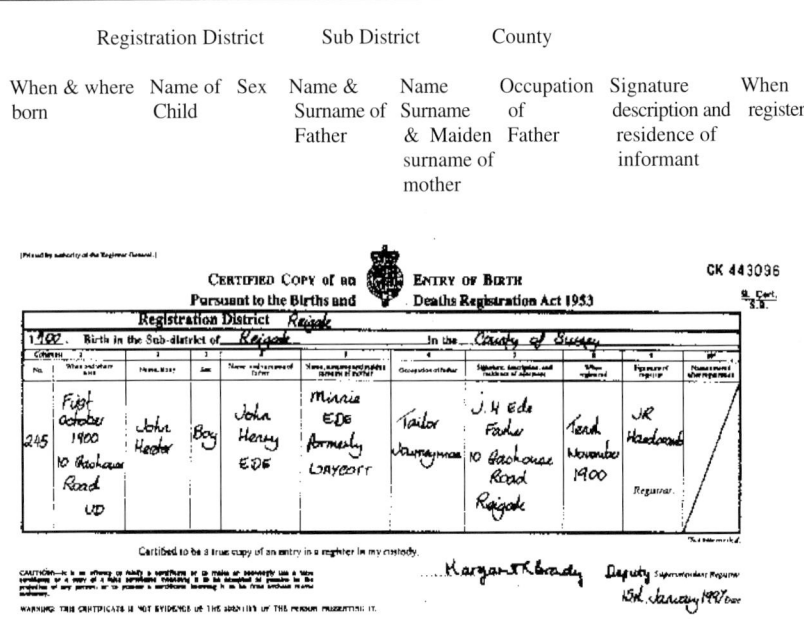

Copyright of the Public Record Office

This should therefore have identified the grandparents and their address at the time of the birth of their child. In searching several years either side of this date in the birth indexes, brothers and sisters birth dates can also be discovered which provides data for the other branches of the family tree.

Death certificates can also be very useful for identifying a birth date as the age at death is given. Again this is not always reliable as it depends on the information the informant has at the time of registration however it does provide a useful pointer. The following information is provided on this certificate:

Example: Death Certificate information provided

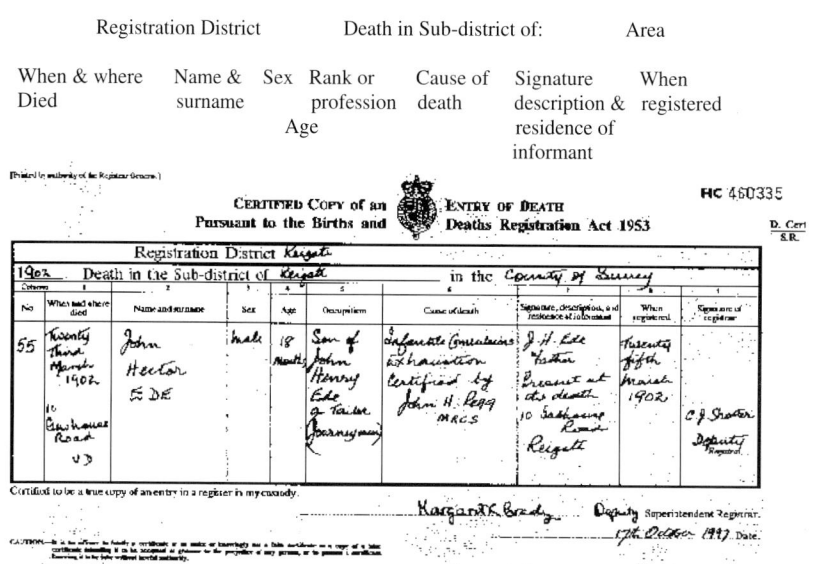

Copyright of the Public Record Office

Whilst looking up the indexes it is wise to note down the index volumes you have looked at and to record any useful data on members of your family as it is discovered. The form shown on the next page is quite useful for this purpose. When looking up the birth indexes it is likely you will also discover the birth dates of brothers and sisters if applicable.

Year	Quarter				Code		Name in full	District
	Dec	Mar	June	Sept.				

When you find an ancestor tick the box of the quarter it was registered and enter the volume and page code in the code boxes followed by the full name in the name box. Enter the registration district. This information will be required when you order the certificate. If you don't find any ancestors in a particular quarter then put a cross in that quarter box. This will avoid going back over books you have already looked at.

Location of Records

	Redhill Library	FHC Woking	PRO Kew	FRC London
Indexes	No	No	Yes	Yes
Certificates	No	No	No	Yes

Chapter Three

Census & Electoral Records

Census records were started in 1801 and then taken every ten years thereafter with the exception of 1941 (Second World War period). The returns up to and including 1831 are of little use to the family historian as the names of residents of each household were not recorded. Those taken from 1841 are however very useful for tracing the whereabouts of whole families. To access these records they normally have to be older than one hundred years, therefore at the time of writing microfilm copies of the 1841; 1851; 1861; 1871; 1881 and 1891 records are available for public access covering England & Wales and the offshore islands at the PRO Family Record Centre in London. County Record offices hold microfilm/fiche copies of those applicable to their own county and a number of Local Studies and lending libraries hold microfilm/fiche copies of those covering local districts.

The 1841 census typically provides the following information:
- City or Borough and Parish or Township
- Street/Road name, place or number of house
- Name and Surname of each person in the house on census day
- Age and Sex of occupants, normally rounded down to nearest five years except in case of under fifteen years of age which were required to be accurate.
- Profession Trade Employment or Independent means.
- Whether born in same County
- Whether born in Scotland or Foreign parts

Example of 1841 enumerators return

Parish of Buckland

PLACE	HOUSES		NAMES of each Person who abode therein the preceding Night	AGE and SEX		PROFESSION, TRADE, EMPLOYMENT, or INDEPENDENT MEANS	Where Born	
			Joseph Hutchens	15			n	
			George do	15			n	
			Mary Anne do		15		n	
			Lucy do		13		n	
			Charlotte do		11		n	
			Ann do		9		n	
			Emma do		7		n	
			Arthur do	5			n	
			Edward Davis	15		M.S.	n	
Lawrence's Farm		1	James Field	45		Farmer	y	
			William Barrer	20		M.S.	y	
			Mary Ann Newell		30	F.S.	y	
			Jane Nightingale		15	F.S.	y	
Upper Green		1	William Bate	40		Ag. Lab.	y	
			Mary do		35		n	
			Emily do		15		y	
			Maria do		10		y	
			William do	7			y	
			Alfred do	7			y	
			James do	5			y	
			George do	7m			y	
			James Reed	55		Ag. Lab.	y	
			John Cullen	40		Ag. Lab.	n	
			William Henley	20		Ag. Lab.	n	
TOTALS Page 12	2			14	10		15	14

Copyright of the Public Record Office

The 1851 return format was revised as shown below. A significant improvement in required information was added which included the relationship to the head of the family, condition of matrimonial status ie, married, single, widowed, age of each person, Occupation, place of birth ie, parish and county of birth and whether blind, deaf and dumb. In the 1871 returns it was also required to indicate whether a person was an imbecile, idiot or lunatic. Other minor changes occurred for each decade.

The place of birth in particular provides a very important linkage pointer as it was quite common for families to move from their original parish in order to seek employment. The coming of the railways and the depression on the farms did much to accelerate this process.

Example of 1851 enumerators return

Copyright of the Public Record Office

It should be noted that many local history groups across the country have been busy name indexing the 1851 and other censuses. The 1881 Census has been indexed as part of a major project involving the Public Record Office, the Mormons and the Federation of Family History Societies and is available on CDs in many record offices. It is therefore well worth checking for the existence of these name indexes for the area you are interested in, as it can save a great deal of time searching through hundreds of pages of census returns. Name indexes are in alphabetical order which are linked with relevant PRO piece, folio and page number. At the time of writing the Reigate & District Family History Group had started a project to index the 1891 Census for the Reigate area.

Location of Census Records for Reigate & District

Census	Redhill Library	FHC Woking	PRO Kew	FRC London
1841	Y	Y	Y	Y
1851	Y	Y	Y	Y
1861	Y	Y	Y	Y
1871	Y	Y	Y	Y
1881	Y	Y	Y	Y
1891	Y	Y	Y	Y

The parishes included in the Reigate & District returns typically: includes: Reigate foreign, Reigate, Redhill, St Johns, Earlswood, Gatton, Merstham, Nutfield, Bletchingley, Leigh, Buckland, Betchworth & Brockham.

A Clearer Sense of the Census 1996 (PRO handbook 28) is recommended reading for a detailed explanation of the census returns.

PRO References

Class Reference	Years
HO 107	1841 & 1851
RG 9	1861
RG 10	1871
RG 11	1881
RG 12	1891
RG 13*	1901

* Currently closed to public inspection.

Electoral Registers

Knowing the address of the person you are researching can save a great deal of time when looking up the census returns. If this has not been previously identified from civil registration certificates or family sources then Electoral Registers could provide the means of locating this information. Jeremy Gibson & Colin Rogers booklet - *Electoral Registers since 1832 and Burgess Rolls* highlight those qualified to vote and how this changed with time to include increasing numbers of voters:

The development of Parliamentary reform and male representation from 1832 to 1918 (or 1928 for woman) is complicated. A distinction was made between those qualifying to vote in county and borough seats, between freehold owners of property, those with copyhold and ordinary tenants. People voted where they qualified to vote which was not always where they lived and some people qualified for more than one vote.

To find who might have qualified for a vote and so might appear on the electoral registers or in the poll books read Gibson and Rogers' booklet already mentioned or you may find a number of other useful history books dealing with electoral reform in the nineteenth century in your local library.

Location of Local Electoral Register

Jeremy Gibson's guide previously noted identifies the main location of electoral registers for each county. The Surrey electoral registers are held at Surrey History Service Centre, Woking. A copy of the 1875 East Surrey Electoral Register on roll film is held at Redhill Library which includes many parishes. Those adjacent to and including Reigate are listed below:

Betchworth	Buckland	Carshalton	Gatton	Headley
Leigh	Merstham	Nutfield	Reigate	Kingswood

Example Part of Reigate Foreign 1875 Electoral Register

POLLING DISTRICT OF REIGATE.

FOREIGN OF REIGATE.

To Poll at Balterness	No.	Christian Name and Surname of each Voter at full length	Place of Abode	Nature of Qualification	Street, Lane, or other like Place in this Township and Number of House (if any) or Property Qualifications, or Name of the Property, by any, or Name of the occupying Tenant. Qualification consists of a Rent charge. Names of the Owners of the Property on such rent is issuing, or names of three, and the of his Property.
	8110	*Agate, Major	Beulah hill, Norwood. S.E.	Freehold land	North road
	8110	Alexander, George William	Woodhatch, Reigate, Surrey	Freehold house	Allingham road, Holmesdale George Sandford, tenant
	8111	Apps, William Wells	Garland road, Red hill	Freehold houses	Garland road, Red hill
	8112	Apted, Oliver Cromwell	High street, Reigate	Two freehold houses	Somerset road, Meadvale, occ. Edmund Comber, and anoth.
	8113	Ash, Rev. John George Hale	Beachley vicarage, Chepstow, Gloucestershire	Two freehold houses	High Field lodge and Glover London road
	8114	Atfield, Charles	Brighton road, Redhill	Freehold house	Brighton road
	8115	Backhouse, Frederick William	Chart lodge, Redstone, Redhill	Occupation of house	Near Redstone
	8116	Bailey, Charles	Buckhurst, Redhill	Leasehold house	Buckhurst
	8117	Balfour, Jabez Spencer	85, London road, Croydon	Freehold land and houses	Holmesdale road
	8118	Balfour, James	Talfourd villa, Holmesdale road, Reigate	Freehold land, coach house, and stable	Adjoining Talfourd villa, let Spencer Balfour
	8119	Batchelor, John	Old Golden Cross, Hastings	Four freehold cottages and gardens	Garlands road, Redhill, Surrey
	8120	Baxter, Robert Cordy	Gatton road, Wray park, Reigate	Occupation of house	Gatton road, Wray park

Copyright of Surrey History Service

Chapter Four

Church of England Parish Registers

Parish registration of baptism, marriage and burials was started in the reign of Henry VIII, 1538. Unfortunately not many registers have survived back to that time and those that have are likely to be in a poor state and difficult to read. In 1598 an order was made that a copy had to be made by each incumbent of all registrations recorded for the previous year and sent to the Bishop. These were known as Bishops transcripts. This practise continued to the present time and provides a valuable alternative source for these records.

In general the majority of pre 1900 parish records will have been deposited with the approved Diocesan repository, usually the local County Record Office for safe keeping and as such will be available for viewing by the general public. In some cases the original register books will be made available. Many have now been copied onto roll film or microfiche in order to preserve the originals and hence it may be necessary to book a viewer before attending the record office. It is always wise to check before going that the record you want to view is available.

A number of pre 1900 parish registers have not been deposited with the record offices and hence it will be necessary to contact the relevant vicar to request permission to view. Where this permission is granted it is appreciated by the incumbent if a small donation is put in the church fund, this also makes it easier to return for a further search if necessary. If a search is requested by post then a small contribution should be sent by way of appreciation. This is helpful to other genealogists who may approach the same incumbent for help with their research in the future.

Parish Register Examples

Up to 1754 for marriages and 1812 for baptism's and burials there had been no standard format formalised for these registers and hence content and layout varied from parish to parish.

Extract from 1759/60 Buckland Baptism Register.

Copyright of Surrey History Service

It was fairly common with these early registers for baptisms to be recorded on one page and marriages and burials on other pages, however in a number of these registers baptisms marriages and burials have been recorded on the same page in the order in which they occurred. It can be seen from the example that they can be quite difficult to read. Marriage indexes for pre 1754 marriages could provide an alternative source that should be explored.

Marriage registration standard format from 1754

Introduced by the Hardwicke Act in 1754 required that a marriage could only legally take place after the calling of banns in the parish church, normally the bride's , or by marriage licence which tended to be preferred by the wealthier.

Copyright of Surrey History Service

Baptism and Burial registration from 1812

The Rose Act of 1812 established for the first time a standard printed format for these registers which are very easy to read and provide much useful information as can be seen from the Baptism example below.

Copyright of Surrey History Service

Burials took on a similar format and provide such data as name of deceased, abode, date of burial, age at death and who performed the ceremony. They will also identify in which parish, county and year the burial occurred.

Subsequent to the 1st of July 1837 the Anglican marriage register took on a similar format to the actual civil registration certificate, with two marriage entries for each page as shown below.

Post 1837 Marriage Register

Copyright of Surrey History Service

Microfilm copies of local Parish Registers held at Redhill Library

Town/ Village	Parish	Baptism	Banns	Marriage	Burials
Bletchingley	St Mary	1538-1812 1812-1906		1538-1812 1754-1923	1538-1812 1813-1910
Buckland	St Mary	1560-1890	1821-1895	1560-1877	1560-1900
Gatton	St Andrew	1599-1754 1813-1882	1754-1812	1599-1900	1599-1754 1813-1883
Godstone *	St Nicholas	1662-1812			1662-1812
Leigh	St Bartholomew	1579-1900	1754-1812	1581-1900	1599-1900
Merstham	St Katherine	1538-1783 1813-1875	1755-1836	1540-1901	1538-1900
Nutfield	St Peter & St Paul	1558-1906	1754-1812	1558-1900	1558-1877
Redhill	St John	1843-1900		1848-1875	1843-187
Redhill	St Matthews	1866-1903		1867-1909	
Reigate	St Mary	1556-1610 1610-1627 1627-1667 1653-1665 1655-1665 1666-1679 1654-1766 1667-1812		1556-1610 1610-1627 1627-1667 1655-1665 1666-1679 1654-1766	1560-16 1610-16 1627-16 1653-16 1666-16 1654-17 1767-18
Tandridge *		1666-1840			1695-1

* The Godstone & Tandridge records are name index's.only by Cliff Webb West Surrey Family History Society.

27

Surrey Parish Records held at Surrey History Centre, Woking

A copy of a guide to Parish Registers held at:

Surrey History Centre,
130 Goldsworth Road,
Woking
Tel: (01483) 594594

is available for reference in Redhill Library. This guide indicates that the majority of Surrey Baptism, Marriage and Burial registers are held at Woking in a number of media formats ie, original registers; microfilm copies, photocopies, transcripts or pints. . If you are planning a visit telephone first to reserve a fiche or roll film reader machine, as appropriate. You will need to take your Library card with you to register on arrival and to obtain access to original documents.

As noted previously microfilm copies of local parish records for Reigate and adjacent Parishes are held and maintained in Redhill Library by the Family History Group. Contact the Library to establish the days when the The Redhill Centre for Local & Family History is manned by volunteers.

Chapter Five

Nonconformist & Roman Catholic records

The term 'Dissenter', later replaced by 'Nonconformist' refers to those who refused to adhere to the Church of England after the Restoration in 1660, and those who left it after the passing of the Act of Uniformity in 1662. There were four main groups: Presbyterians believed in a national church but without bishops; Independents believed in the independence of each congregation; Baptists were like Independents but did not believe in infant baptism; and the Society of Friends (Quakers) did not have sacraments and rejected the church establishment to the extent of refusing to pay tithes and church rates.

The Act of Toleration 1689 allowed these groups freedom of worship provided that they registered with either Quarter Sessions or the church authorities. Surrey was not a strong Nonconformist county. Most of the main towns had a Dissenting chapel but these fluctuated in strength: Reigate's, for example, was down to eight or ten members in 1833. In villages there might be meetings in private houses. The Presbyterians more or less died out in southern England in the eighteenth century, leaving Independents, Baptists and Quakers. Only the Quakers took seriously the need to preserve records. This was partly because they rejected baptism, church marriage and churchyard burials, whereas until the nineteenth century the other Dissenters were generally baptised and always married in their parish church and buried in the churchyard.

As late as 1851 there were only two Independent chapels and the Society of Friends meeting house in Reigate and in the rest of Reigate registration district there were two Independent chapels - Gadbrook and Charlwood - four Baptist chapels – Brockham, Horley, Outwood and Smallfield – and two mission meetings in Nutfield.

John Wesley, founder of the main Methodist connexion, preached in Surrey from 1740 onwards and his last sermon was preached at Leatherhead a week before his death in 1791. He intended his movement to remain with the Church of England but in practice it had become a separate denomination before the end of the eighteenth century. There were various schisms within Methodism, of which the Primitive Methodists, originating in 1808, were the only denomination to be found extensively in Surrey, In 1851 there were no Methodist chapels in Reigate registration district. Nonconformity expanded in the Victorian age, and most surviving chapels and their records date from no earlier than that period. The Presbyterians reappeared, mainly because of Scots migrating to England. The Presbyterians and most Congregationalists united in 1972 to create the United Reformed Church; most Surrey URC churches were formerly Congregational.

The best brief introduction to Nonconformist history and records is M.Mullett, *Sources for the history of English Nonconformity, 1660-1830* (British Records Association, Archives and the User, 1991).Nonconformist family history sources are described in detail in D J Steel, *Sources for Nonconformist Genealogy and Family History* (National Index of Parish Registers vol.2 1973). A register of births was kept from 1743 to 1837 and is held at Dr Williams's Library, Gordon Square, London, which holds many other Nonconformist records and publications. Many chapel registers between 1775 and 1837 are accessible on microfilm at the Family Records Centre in London. Records of many Surrey chapels are held at Surrey History Centre. These only occasionally include registers but they often include lists of members. Many others remain in the chapels.

A useful indication of Nonconformist presence in eighteenth-century Surrey can be found in *Parson and Parish in Eighteenth-Century Surrey: Replies to Bishops' Visitations* (Surrey Record Society, 1994) and for 1851 in *The 1851 Religious Census: Surrey* (Surrey Record Society, 1997). Meeting house certificates can be found at Surrey History Centre, Woking, for Quarter Sessions registration and at London Metropolitan Archives for registrations in the archdeaconry court.

Roman Catholicism

After Henry VIII's break with Rome, and more particularly after the death of Mary in 1558, there were men and women, often called 'recusants', who adhered to the 'old religion' and remained loyal to the Roman Catholic church. They were persecuted severely in the sixteenth and seventeenth centuries and continued to suffer various disabilities until the nineteenth century. From the 1720s they were generally free in practice to worship and the Catholic Relief Acts of 1778 and 1791 removed the most serious penal laws; under the 1791 Act Catholic chapels were required to be registered and thus became legal. Many of these were centred on individual families and lacked continuity. The revival of Roman Catholicism dates from Irish immigration in the late eighteenth and nineteenth centuries. Surrey had a number of important 'recusant' families including the Copleys of Gatton and Westons of Sutton but as late as 1851 there were only two churches in Surrey outside what is now Greater London: at Weybridge and Sutton Place. During the later part of the century and during the twentieth century they expanded dramatically. Sources for Roman Catholic churches are in various places. Many are probably still held in the churches. D J Steel and E.R.Samuel, *Sources for Roman Catholic and Jewish Genealogy and Family History* (National Index of Parish Registers vol.3.1974) is a very helpful guide.

The Surrey Record Society works quoted above will be found helpful also for Roman Catholicism.

It is also suggested that the most useful publications of the Catholic Record Society can be consulted in the library at the Society of Genealogists in London.

Huguenots

The main immigration of Huguenots to England from France followed the Revocation of the Edict of Nantes which took place in 1685. Copies of registers are held in the Library at the Family Records Centre London.

Jews

Outside London and major cities Jewish settlement was rare before the late nineteenth centuries. Local synagogues may be able to assist the researcher and the work by D J Steel and E R Samuel quoted above will be found extremely useful.

Chapter Six

Churches, Cemeteries and Graveyards

The churches and chapels reviewed in this chapter are local to Reigate and surrounding districts, some of the churches have records going back to the late 1500s whereas the chapels tend to originate from the eighteenth or nineteenth century. All of the Churches and many of the chapels are still in use today. The Parishes included are limited to Reigate, Redhill, Gatton, Merstham, Nutfield, Bletchingley, Leigh, Sidlow, Buckland and Betchworth.

Church of England Churches

Betchworth
St Michael

This is a surprisingly large church for a small village, this is probably because at one time it served both Betchworth and Brockham, at least up to the time Brockham Parish was created (1847). A brief but interesting history of the church with a diagram dating the different sections of the building with a guide tour is available at the visitors table for a small donation, this notes that the earliest reference to the church can be found in the Domesday book of 1086, indicating pre conquest origins. Mounted on one of the interior walls is a list of serving vicars going back to 1286 when William of Merstham was the first appointed vicar. A large parish chest hewn out of a solid oak tree trunk that housed the parish records up to the present century will be of interest to family history visitors in particular. Its age is not known however the church history notes state that the tree may have been alive at the time of Christ. Major restoration work took place in 1851 and 1870. The only parts of the Norman Church which remain are the western arch.

With regard to the monumental inscriptions within the adjacent graveyard the earliest readable stones appear to date from 1767 up to 1997 which includes a war memorial to those of the parish who gave their lives in both the 1914-19 and 1939-45 wars. There is an overflow graveyard a few hundred yards away with stones dating from 1951 to the present time.

The following Registers are held by the Surrey History Centre, Woking:

Register Type	Baptism	Marriage	Burial
Original	1558-1885	1562-1837	1558-1893
Microfilm	1558-1885	1562-1837	1558-1893
Photocopy	1810-1885		
Transcript	1837-1885	1837-1925	

Buckland
St Mary the Virgin

Located on the Reigate to Dorking road. Ian Nairn's book *The Building of England Surrey* points out that this is one of Woodyer's best achievements. It incorporates the old four post belfry framing and is built of Surrey's attractive Bargate sandstone. There is a 14th Century stained glass window depicting figures of St Peter and St Paul on the north side of the nave. Nairn considers this glass as about the best in the county

Within the church is documented a historical outline of the building by Eric A.Atkinson which can be viewed by visitors. There is also a brief history guide that can purchased for a small sum. A list of vicars appointed from 1308 to the present time is mounted on the wall of the church. Monumental inscriptions in the graveyard that are still readable date from 1760 up to 1997.

The following Registers are held by the Surrey History Centre, Woking:

Register Type	Baptism	Marriage	Burial
Original	1560-1890	1560-1836	1560-1966
Microfilm	1560-1890	1560-1877	1560-1900
Transcript	1560-1837	1660-1836	1560-1837
Banns		1821-1895	

Note: Microfilm copies also held at Redhill Library.

Bletchingley
St Mary the Virgin

This is a very interesting ancient Church, 'well worth a visit', with many helpful historical notes located around the building, one of which indicates that there has been a church on this site for 900 years with the tower claimed to be the oldest part. The lower parts of the tower date from the end of the 11th century. The oak steeple was badly burnt in 1606 from lightning. The present peal of eight bells dates from 1780 and was rehung in 1912 when five bells were recast. In 1908 the tower was restored.

A brief historical and helpful guide is available for visitors located just inside the main entrance. At the base of the tower on the wall are mounted pictures of Henry the VIII, Anne of Cleves, Edward VI and Thomas Cromwell, Secretary of state to Henry VIII. There is also a chart showing the descent of the Manor of Bletchingley.

Near the South Chapel, dedicated to Saint Catherine and Margaret is a hole in the wall facing the village which is believed to be the site of the cell of Brother Roger, Hermit of Bletchingley. There is a fine marble memorial statue (1705) to Sir Robert Clayton, Alderman of the city of London and his wife Dame Martha Clayton and their baby son Robert who died very young. Another interesting tomb within the church is that of Sir Thomas Cawarden, d 1559. He was keeper of the Tents, Toyles and Hales to King Henry VIII and Master of the Revels, he was also Steward to Ann of Cleaves from whom he took over Bletchingley place where he lived in state with 100 liveried servants.

A list of memorial inscriptions transcribed in 1984 from existing gravestones in the churchyard by A.O.Brown is available for consultation in the Church.

St Mark's Church at South Park Bletchingley opened in 1909 with seating for 60 persons.

The following Registers are held by the Surrey History Centre, Woking:

Register Type	Baptism	Marriage	Burial
Original	1538-1986	1538-1986	1538-1978
Microfilm	1538-1906	1538-1923	1538-1910
No Marriages		(1695-1705)	

Note: Microfilm copies also held at Redhill Library.

Gatton
St Andrew

The river Mole has its source in this Parish. From the time of Henry VI (1442-61) until the reform Act of 1832 this place with a population of 145, returned two members to Parliament. The town hall, marking the site of the Borough still stands in Gatton Park. St Andrews Church is a building of stone in the early English style. The tower contains a clock and one bell. A lych gate was erected as a memorial to those who fell in the 1914-18 war.

The following Registers are held by the Surrey History Centre, Woking:

Register Type	Baptism	Marriage	Burial
Original	1599-1986	1599-1973	1599-1992
Microfilm	1599-1882	1599-1900	1599-1883
Transcripts	1813-1841		1813-1841

Note: Microfilm copies also held at Redhill Library.

Gatton
Parish Church-St Andrew (Copy of drawing by John Hassell circa 1809)

Copyright of Surrey History Service

Leigh
St Bartholomew

This parish is on the river Mole, three miles south west of Reigate. The Church contains brasses to the Arderne family, who were owners of Leigh Place. There is a tablet in memory of the eleven men of the Parish who fell in the Great War 1914-18.

The first Rector was appointed in 1262 to the Prior and Canons of Newark in the Parish of Send and services were probably provided by the Canons in the church up to 1567 when the first vicar was appointed, John Rothe.

Monumental inscriptions in this churchyard that have not yet eroded to the point where they cannot be read date from 1724 up to 1997

The following Registers are held by the Surrey History Centre, Woking:

Register Type	Baptism	Marriage	Burial
Original	1597-1919	1581-1976	1599-1906
Microfilm	1579-1900	1581-1900	1599-1906
Transcripts	1579-1838	1581-1838	1579-1838

Note: Microfilm copies also held at Redhill Library.

Merstham
St Katherine

The Church of St Katherine, located on a hill at the east end of the village is built of stone, chiefly in the Early English style and consists of chancel, nave of three bays, aisles, two chapels of the 14th century and a western tower containing a clock and six bells. Reference to the Parish of Merstham dates back to A.D.675. It is likely therefore that a place of worship existed pre conquest. The foundation of this Church is believed to date from the onset of the Anglo Norman period, traceable in the dedication of the Church to St Katherine. The chancel and porch was added between 1450 and 1500. The present building is mainly first half of the 13th century with later additions. The tower dates from c1220. There are monuments within the church to the Jolliffe family and to Nicholas Jamys, chief mercer of the City of London in the 15th century.

The following Registers are held by the Surrey History Centre, Woking:

Register Type	Baptism	Marriage	Burial
Original	1538-1964	1540-1970	1538-1937
Microfilm	1538-1902	1540-1901	1538-1901
Printed	1538-1840	1538-1836	1538-1851

Note: Microfilm copies also held at Redhill Library.

Nutfield
St Peter & St Paul

The Church is located on Church Hill and is built in the early English style There is a war memorial on the west wall, which bears the names of the Nutfield men who gave their lives in both the first and second world wars.

There is a short history guide available in the church which notes the village and church are mentioned in the Domesday book and also highlights the various changes that have taken place with the structure of the church over the different periods.

The following Registers are held by the Surrey History Centre, Woking:

Register Type	Baptism	Marriage	Burial
Original	1558-1906	1558-1924	1558-1913
Microfilm	1558-1906	1558-1900	1558-1913
Printed		1813-1837	

Note: Microfilm copies also held at Redhill Library.

Nutfield Parish Church-St Peter and St Paul

copyright Arthur Hawkes

South Nutfield
Christ Church

In November 1910 part of the Parish of St Peter & St Paul was ecclesiastically annexed to Christ Church to cater for the increasing population of South Nutfield. The Registers of baptism and marriage are held by the incumbent.

Redhill
***St John the Evangelist
Church***

Copyright Arthur Hawkes

St John the Evangelist Church lies on a noll between the junction of Pendleton and Church Road and is an ecclesiastical parish formed in 1844 and built in the Gothic style. This was the first district church in the Borough of Reigate and was built to cater for the growing population of workers who came with the building of the London to Brighton railway. The area became known locally as little London. Of the original fabric little remains as the building was significantly transformed in 1889. The tower with spire was completed in 1895 and contains a peal of eight bells, which were re-hung in 1931. As can be seen below the registers date from 1843.

The following Registers are held by the Surrey History Centre, Woking:

Register Type	Baptism	Marriage	Burial
Original	1843-1990	1848-1988	1843-1905
Microfilm	1843-1900	1848-1876	1843-1876
Banns 1877-1964			

Note: Microfilm copies also held at Redhill Library.

St Matthew (Station Road)

St Matthew's is an ecclesiastical parish, formed in 1867 and is built of Reigate and Bath stone in the Early Decorated style, consisting of a chancel, nave, aisles, transepts and tower with spire containing a clock and a single bell. On the west wall is a memorial to those of the parish who fell in the 1914-18 war.

The following Registers are held by the Surrey History Centre, Woking:

Register Type	Baptism	Marriage	Burial
Original	1866-1932	1867-1954	
Microfilm	1866-1903	1867-1909	
Transcripts			

Note: Microfilm copies also held at Redhill Library.

Holy Trinity (London Road Redhill)

Holy Trinity is an ecclesiastical parish formed in 1907 from the northern part of the parish of St Matthew and located at the junction between Carlton road and London road as a memorial to the Rev.H.Brass, first vicar of St Matthew.

At the time of writing the Baptism and Marriage Registers are held by the incumbent and run from 1907.

Reigate
Parish Church-St Mary Magdalene

copyright Arthur Hawkes

Located off Chart Lane and believed to be one of the oldest Churches in the area dating from the 12th century, and comprising a chancel, with north and south chapels, a nave of five bays, aisles and a tower containing a peal of ten bells. The building has undergone significant alteration and renovation through the ages which has left little of the fabric of the original structure. In 1665 Reigate was stricken by the plague resulting in 107 deaths. The first plague burial in this churchyard was the 31/07/1665 and the last the 14//04/ 1666.

In 1701 Andrew Cranston the vicar at that time established what is known as the Cranston Library, which contains some 1700 volumes of both general and theological books and manuscripts located on the second floor of the vestry. This was the first public library in England, as lending was permitted from its beginning. The Parish registers date from 1556.

The present Cemetery was established in 1855 and later enlarged, adjoins the parish churchyard and extends over about 12 acres. A portion of the ground was set aside for Roman Catholics. This Cemetery is now closed.

The following Registers are held by the Surrey History Centre, Woking:

Register Type	Baptism	Marriage	Burial
Original	1556-1910	1556-1906	1560-1906
Microfilm	1556-1910	1556-1906	1560-1812
Transcripts	1556-1733	1558-1754	1561-1718

Chapel of St Cross (Reigate Heath)

Formerly known as the Mill Chapel having been a mill in earlier years. There is also an iron church on Reigate Heath located at the southern end of the houses down a lane.

St Mark's (Alma Road)

St Marks is an ecclesiastical parish formed in 1860 from the civil parishes of Reigate and Buckland. The registers date from 1860 and are currently held by the incumbent.

St Philip (Nutley Lane)

Erected and endowed in 1864. St Philip is a conventional district church built to cater for the increasing population of Reigate.

St Lukes (South Park)

This again is an ecclesiastical parish formed in 1871 out of Reigate Parish to cater for the increasing population of the South Park region of Reigate. The church is a building in the Gothic style of the 14th century. The registers are currently held by the incumbent.

Sidlow Bridge
Emmanuel Church

An ecclesiastical parish formed in 1862 from a detached part of Buckland parish and from the parishes of Charlwood, Horley, Leigh and Reigate. It lies adjacent to the river Mole on the old Brighton Road. Built in the Early English style with flint stone dressing. Registers date from 1862 and are held by the incumbent at the time of writing.

OTHER DENOMINATIONS
Roman Catholic Churches
Redhill
St Joseph's (Ladbroke Road formally High St. Consecrated in 1898)

Reigate
Church of Holy Family (York Road) Opened in 1938.
St Michael's (Cockshot Hill)

Merstham
St Teresa (Weldon Way)

Methodist Churches
Bletchingley
Baptism Register 1874-1991 held at Surrey History Centre, Woking. File Ref. (*SHC 4525/1/1*)

Meadvale
Lower Road

Redhill
Gloucester Road

Brighton Road (Demolished) marriage register 1911-1952 held at Surrey History Centre, Woking. Ref. (*SHC 2155/22*)

Reigate
High Street

Lesbourne Road (Primitive Methodists) marriage registers 1941-1943 held at Surrey History Centre, Woking. Ref. (*SHC 2155/21*)

Baptist Churches
Earlswood
St Johns Road

Merstham
Weldon Way

Redhill
Hatchlands Road

Reigate
Reigate Priory School

Presbyterians/Congregationalists/United Reformed Church
Redhill (Built 1902)
St Paul's - Shaws Corner, Hatchlands Road

Reigate Congregational Church
(High Street) Reigate marriage registers 1940-1972 held at Surrey *History* Centre, Woking. Ref. (*SHC 6530/8-12*)

Allingham Road South Park

Other Cemeteries in the Locality
Redstone Cemetery - Philanthropic Rd Redhill
This cemetery opened in 1932. Burial registers are held at the Redstone site office and include burials at both Redstone and Chart Lane burial grounds, (Chart Lane burial ground is adjacent to St Mary's Church graveyard and is segregated by a footpath). Records are held on computer and searches can be carried out, by contacting the Redstone Office. Tel.(01737) 761592.

There is a search fee at the present time. Cremations where the ashes are buried at Redstone will also be held on record, but these are currently not on the computer and it may take longer to access specific names. It should be noted that the Redstone Cemetery includes allocated sections for Catholic and other denomination burials as well as Church of England.

Nutfield Road
Nutfield parish overflow burial ground is located between Redhill and Nutfield, next to the old Fullers Earth works. Earliest memorial stones at this site date from 1889.

Burial Registers for St Peter & St Paul's Parish from 1558 to 1913 are held at the Surrey History Centre, Woking with microfilm copies 1558 to 1913 held at Redhill Library. Later records are held by the incumbent.

Godstone Road

Bletchingley St Mary's overflow burial grounds are located on the Godstone side of Bletchingley village, opposite Rabies Heath Road. Earliest memorial stones at this site date from 1859.

Burial Registers for St Mary's from 1538 to 1978 are held by the Surrey History Centre, Woking with microfilm copies 1813 to 1910 available at Redhill Library. Burial records, later than 1978 are held by the incumbent. Indexes to all Births Marriages and Deaths within the UK from 1837, as noted previously are available for public access at the Family Record Centre London.

Cremation Records

Cremation records are held by the crematorium, where the cremation took place. The Surrey & Sussex Crematorium is located in Balcombe Road, Horley, RH10. Tel.(01293) 888930 & 882345 serves the local area of Reigate & District as well as other Surrey & Sussex areas. This crematorium opened in 1956.

Chapter Seven

School Records

The rise and development of the National School system was effectively launched by the 1870 elementary education Act and the building of National Board Schools which followed. Long before that however schools existed, not just for the wealthy but also for poor children in the western world. The ancient Greeks were credited as the cradle of western education and as the starting place of its history back in the 4th and 5th century BC. The Greeks regarded education as a major service of the State and essential instrument for the training of its citizens. By 1500 as many as 79 universities had been founded in Europe and in many parts of Western Europe there were soon established Schools usually for boys and often run by religious foundations. Religion and Latin formed the main part of the curriculum.

The reformation had a disruptive influence on English education. The job of education was now taken on largely by charitable foundations and wealthy philanthropists, most famously Edward VI. Schools providing an elementary education for the lower orders of society were few and usually inadequate and in the 18th century education for the masses was generally regarded as undesirable, even dangerous. There was, however, from the beginning of the 19th century a gradual acceptance that some education for all children would be good for the industrial economy. The Established Church and in a few cases the nonconformist churches also began to appreciate the importance of primary education and many 'ordinary' schools grew out of Sunday Schools from which adults as well as children could benefit. One of the big debates of the last part of the nineteenth century was the perceived threat to the moral welfare of the country if the job of education were to be taken out of the hands of religious bodies and handed over to the secular authorities. But by the end of the century the government had largely taken responsibility for administration of the education of the working classes.

Existing School Records
School records tend to be log books, admission registers or sporting event records, sometimes including photographs. A number of these have been deposited with the Surrey History Centre, Woking and are noted against specific schools as appropriate. If the records are not at Woking then a direct approach to the head of the school of interest is recommended. The log books tend to be a diary of school administration and events, they often refer to teachers by name but there is normally no reference to pupils by individual names unless there has been a serious breach of discipline, such as repeated absenteeism. The admission registers normally record when pupils join and leave the school.

Buckland
Church of England Primary School *(Mixed & Infants)*

Bletchingley
County Primary School *(Junior, mixed & Infants)*

St Katherine's Secondary School (*Surrey County Council*) Godstone Road.

Gatton
Royal Alexandra & Albert School and Gatton County Secondary
Ref. *(SHC 6129/4/1-90)* Surrey History Centre

School records including minutes, pupil records, estate records and photographs.

Leigh
County Primary School *(Mixed & Infants)* Tapners Road
Burys Court Boys Preparatory School *(Private)*

Merstham
County Primary School (Boys & Girls)
County Primary School (Infants)

Formally village school. An excellent book on the village school, entitled *The History of Merstham School* has been written by John Neal, Printed & Published by Wine Press. Copy in Redhill Library.

Nutfield
Nutfield Priory School
Surrey History Center, Woking Ref. *(SHC 3433)*
Records including governors' minutes 1976-87, Year Books 1961-1970s, staff meeting minutes 1956-86, attendance registers 1965-87, files relating to curriculum 1955-75, and school magazines 1979-85.

Primary School (Mixed & Infants)

South Nutfield
Primary School (Infants*)*

Redhill
St John's Meadvale School
Ref. (*SHC CES/75/1)*
1   Log Book   May 1906-May 1916

St John's County Primary Boys School
Ref. (*SHC CES/81)*
1   Log Book   Aug 1954-Jul 1964

Redhill Junior (Secondary) Technical School
Started 1926 later became Redhill Secondary School (1955). Finally Redhill Technical School. Closed 1963. Last student left 1966
Tom Slaughter's book*, The History of Redhill Junior Technical School* covers this in detail with reference to staff and pupils who attended.

Redhill Wesleyan School (Cromwell Road)
Jan-Dec 1885 Girls. Mixed April 1872 - Jan 1909 then transferred to Local Education Authority 1909 4th Feb. Later Cromwell Road Elementary School, later Long Mead First School.

1	Log Book	1872-1955

Building demolished in 1902 and replaced by Cromwell Road Elementary School on same site. Opened in 1910. Surrey County Council School set up in 1947. Closed 1955.

Wesleyan Infants School
Ref. (*SHC* C/ES/76) Family History Centre, Woking
1	Log Book		Jan 1881-Dec 1894
2	 " "		Jan 1895-Dec 1909

St Mathew's National Boys School (Station Road)
Built in 1872 for 270 boys. The girls & Infants school built in 1884 on the site of the old church, which from 1866 had been used as a girls & infants school, and held 254 girls & 251 infants.
Ref. (*SHC* C/ES/77)
1	Log Book		Feb 1889-May 1905
2	 " "		May 1905-Oct 1918
3	 " "		Oct 1918-May 1959

Frenches Road Boys School
(later Frenches County Secondary mixed school 1947-1955)
(later Frenches County Secondary Boys School)
Ref. (*SHC C/ES/78*)
1	Log Book		Sep 1906-Dec 1937
2	 " "		Jan 1938-Jul 1963
3	Miscellany found in log book /2 including photograph, newspaper cuttings, speech day proceedings

Frenches Road Girls School
Ref. (*SHC C/ES/79*)
1   Log Book   Sep 1906-Dec 1932
2   Log Book   Jan 1933- Sep 1947

Frenches Road Infants School
Ref. (*SHC C/ES/80*)
1   Log Book   1921-1954
1   Log Book   1954-1969

Frenches Road School

copyright Arthur Hawkes

Warwick School Redhill
Ref. (*SHC CC780*)   Governors Minutes

Redstone Secondary School
Ref . (*SHC 3360*)
1   Admission Register   1963-1966
2   Admission Register   1966-1970

3	"	"	1970-1976
4	"	"	1976-1981
5	"	"	1981-1984

Royal Philanthropic Society School Redhill (1788 - 1988)
Ref. (*SHC 3521*)
Records include registers, pupil files, accounts and pictures, order of service for bicentenary of the Society.

Royal Philanthropic Society and Farm school records.
Ref. (*SHC 2271,2524*)

St Joseph Catholic, Brighton Road
Refer to booklet entitled: *St Joseph's Catholic Parish 1855-1955* copy in Redhill Library.

St Nicholas Special School for boys (London Road Redhill)
Formally Police Orphanage

Reigate
Grammar School
The school now known as Reigate Grammar originally started as a free school for the poor children of Reigate. Doctor Ridgeway's notes on the History of Reigate circa 1814 states that in the year 1675 a parcel of land about one acre in size was purchased and a schoolhouse built, with a stock of money which the Parishioners of Reigate Parish then had, and contributions of several gentlemen, but chiefly with money coming to the parish as a legacy of Henry Smith Esq. Silversmith and Alderman of the City of London. The purchase was made under the care of Sir Edward Thurland of Great Doods.

Wilfred Hooper in his book *Reigate through the Ages* devotes a whole chapter to the detailed historical development of this school and points out that it does not appear to have opened until 1684 with the appointment of Rev. John Williamson as Master.

Reigate Free School 1822. Photo of watercolour by J.Hassel

Copyright of Surrey History Service

St Mark's Girls & Infants School
Ref. (*SHC C/ES/69*)
1	Log Book	July 1867-June 1898
2	Log Book	June 1898-1919
3	Log Book	April 1919- 1950
4	Log Book	Nov.1950-Aug 1951
5	Admission Register	boys 1867-1879
		girls 1864-1878
6	Admission Register	1879-1907

St Mark's Infant School
Ref. (*SHC C/ES/69*)
1	Log Book	Sept. 1879- Jul.1909
2	Log Book	Aug. 1909-May 1931
3	Log Book	May 1931-Aug 1933
4	Admission Register	1879-1907
5	Admission Register	1907-1933

St Mark's Boys School
Ref. (*SHC C/ES/70*)
1	Log Book	Jan	1869-Oct.1892
2	Log Book	Nov	1892-Aug1911

St Lukes Infants National, Allingham Road South Park
Ref. (*SHC C/ES/71*)
1	Log Book for Minutes	1873-1876; 1877-1908 see /3 below
2	Log Book	1908-1921

St Luke's Mixed School, later CP (South Park)
From 1889 to 1892 the mixed school was divided into a boys and girls school. Closed in 1972.

3	Log Book	1873-1892
4	"	1892-1907
5	"	1908-1934
6	"	1934-1965
7	"	1965-1972
8	Admission Register	1910-1928
9	"	1928-1938
10	"	1938-1944
11	"	1945-1953
12	"	1966-1972
15	Sports Day Programme & Results	1957-1972
19	Papers relating to sports including photographs of teams	1958-1959

Reigate National Infants School, London Road.

Built 1854 for 380 pupils. Attendance 1891 was 84 boys, 90 girls, 70 infants. Thomas Painter Master, Miss A Parson Mistress, Miss Mines Infants Mistress.

reproduced with approval of The British Library

Ref. (*SHC C/ES/72*)
1	Log Book	Jun.1879-Jun 1896
2	Log Book	Jul 1896-Dec 1923

Lesbourne Lands National (Infants) Effingham Road

Built 1880 for 108 children, average attendance 88. Later Lesbourne Lands Church of England Primary School.

Ref. (*SHC C/ES/73*)
1	Log Book	Sep 1880-Jan 1890
2	" "	Jan 1890-Jan 1906
3	" "	Feb 1906-Nov 1949
4	" "	Nov 1949-Jul 1959

Reigate Parish Church of England Girls School
Ref. (*SHC C/ES/74*)
1   Log Book   Jan 1877-Mar 1904
2   "   "   Apr 1904-Mar 1919

St Mark's National, Holmesdale Road

Built 1869 for 300 children. Average attendance 84 boys, 86 girls, 59 infants. William Punton Master, Miss Kirby Mistress, Miss Rosina Haines Infants Mistress.

British School, High Street Reigate

Built 1852 for 150 children, enlarged in 1888 for 300 Average attendance 170.

Chapter Eight

International Genealogical Index

The International Genealogical Index (IGI) is an important source of information that has been produced by the Family History Library of the Church of Jesus Christ of Latter Day Saints (LDS), (The Mormons). This is an index of millions of entries, predominately baptisms and marriages, mostly taken from parish registers as part of an organised transcription programme concerned with the religious belief of this organisation. In the early days this was called the C.F.I = The Computer File Index.

These indexes are particularly useful as a location tool when there is uncertainty where an ancestor came from. Depression on the farms and the coming of the railways created conditions that encouraged our ancestors to seek work in other parts of the country, county or towns in order to be able to support their families, hence it was quite common for our ancestors to move home frequently. If an individual cannot be found in these records it may be that the parish where they lived has not been transcribed yet for various reasons, also there are gaps.

These records must also be treated with caution as they are subject to error by the nature of the transcription process. It is therefore important to check findings with original source records.

The IGI is a world wide index so it is also useful for tracing ancestors who have emigrated.

The IGI is organised by country, county, parish and names in alphabetic order, so it is fairly easy to home in on the area of interest. There are few entries after 1837. Eve McLaughlin's Guide, *Making the most of the IGI* explains this index in some detail and is well worth consulting.

Typical Example of Extract from IGI Index

Reprinted with permission. Copyright 1992 by Intellectual Reserve, Inc. "Some material in this publication is reprinted by permission of the Church of Jesus Christ of Latter-day Saints. In granting permission for this use of copyrighted material, the Church does not imply or express either endorsement or authorisation of this publication."

Data Layout
Top Band: Country, County, Page Number

Column
1   Name of individual

2   Parents name or spouse of individual

3   Sex -   M   Male
                           F   Female
        Relationship   H   Husband
                           W   Wife

4   Event   A   Adult Christening
                        B   Birth
                        C   Christening
                        D   Death/Burial
                        F   Birth or Christening of first known child (In lieu of marriage date)
                        M   Marriage
                        N   Census
                        S   Miscellaneous
                        W   Will or Probate

5   Date of event

6   Place of event (Town/Parish)

7,8,9   LDS Data only ie, B: Date of baptism; S: Sealing; E: Endowment.

10,11   Source of record. Eve McLaughlin's booklet page 7 describes how to decipher these numbers.

Where to Access the IGI data

The Redhill Centre for Local & Family History hold the 1988 version of the IGI for most counties in England.

The latest version of the IGI is available for access at any of the LDS Family History Centres on compact disc and microfiche. There are also copies available at the Family Record Centre London, PRO Kew and the Surrey History Centre, Woking. The majority of Family History Centres now hold CD-ROM FamilySearch, a computerised version of the IGI. This can also be accessed via Internet. http://www.familysearch.com

A list of LDS Family History Centres in the UK can be obtained from the Internet on:
http://midas.ac.uk/genuki/big/LDS/centres.txt.

Other helpful advice on LDS centres can be obtained from :
http://www.oz.net/~markhow/uksearch.htm entitled: Researching ancestors from the United Kingdom using the LDS Family History Centre resources.

The nearest LDS Family History Centre to Reigate is the Mormon Chapel in Old Horsham Road, Crawley.
Tel (01293) 516151 to make a booking.

Chapter Nine

Wills and Administrations

Probate records are yet another valuable source of family history information which is not easily available from other sources. They can provide details of the deceased's wealth at the time of death, his or her position and status in life as well as profession/trade or skill. The bequests made in such documents are particularly useful in identifying daughters married surnames or son's wife's Christian names. The address of the deceased is given and where there is ownership of property or business this may also be detailed. The original probate records may be held with other interesting documents such as insurance policies, investment details etc. In some cases legacies are left in trust to grandchildren.

Pre January 1858 wills were proved in the ecclesiastical courts of the Church of England, of which there were several hundred. Tracing the court that proved a particular will can be difficult and therefore reference to: *A Simplified Guide to PROBATE JURISDICTION Where to look for Wills* by J.S.W Gibson and *Wills before 1858* by Eve McLaughlin, is recommended.

In general however Surrey was covered by the Prerogative Court of Canterbury (PCC) as was most of the south which meant that the majority of wills in the south were proved in the London courts. Some wills however may have been proved in local courts.

The content of a will as proved in an ecclesiastical court dealt only with personal estate. The local Manor Court dealt with the disposal of real estate such as houses, out buildings and land.

Probate records of the P.C.C can be read at the Family Record Centre, 1 Myddelton Street, EC1R 1UW, London or at the PRO Kew. Jane Cox & Stella Colwell in their book *Never Been Here Before* PRO Readers' Guide No.17, advise however that if you are going to Kew it is better to read them there as the related probate records are also kept at that location.

If a person died without making a will (Intestacy), their estate was divided between the relatives according to certain rules. Where a will has not been made there is likely to be an administration which will provide some useful information but not as much as the will.

The Court of Probate Act 1857 transferred the jurisdiction of all ecclesiastical, royal, peculiar and manorial courts to the court of probate. Eve McLaughlin booklet *Somerset House Wills from 1858* notes that wills dating from January 1858 have been proved in civil courts - either the Principal Probate Registry in London, or the offices of the District Probate Registry. The indexes to these will however until recently were available for reference at Somerset House in the Strand London.

In the July 1998 Reigate & District Family History Group Newsletter R.Furniss published an article indicating that Somerset House (Wills) have been relocated to First Avenue House, 42-49 High Holborn near Chancery Lane tube station (Central Line). Wills dating from 1858 are available for inspection and can be ordered by searching through the many index books (annual). On finding the name, Probate number and Registration District it is necessary to fill in two application forms; one for the will and one for the Probate. Present the completed forms at the desk together with the Index Book and request INSPECTION of the documents which will be produced within one hour. If copies are required pay the fee and these will be posted to you in about one week. Note Indexes 1997 onwards are on microfiche.

Chapter Ten

Taxation Records

Taxation has been around from the earliest times, it was used initially as the means of raising revenue for the Monarch to cover the costs of debts incurred through the Crusades and other wars. It was imposed through the judicial system and became part of the law of the land.

These taxes were imposed on land, property, movable goods etc. In 1188 a tax of one tenth was imposed on land rent and goods. From 1270 responsibility for assessment and collection of this taxation was placed under the control of the exchequer. Taxation was divided between each of the hundreds of the county. Each hundred being further sub-divided into geographical areas of tax collection called wapentakes, towns and boroughs etc.

Lay Subsidy
The Lay subsidy of 1296 was one of the earliest taxes levied on moveable personal wealth where the return records still survive. This tax was paid by laymen (non clergy).

About 1334 fixed shire and borough tax levels were established which continued to be levied until 1624, these varied between 1/15 of the value of the assessment for Shires and 1/10 for towns.

From 1334 until 1523 other taxes were also levied, the most notable being the Poll Tax of 1377. Everyone at the age of 14 years and over was liable. This changed in 1379 to those over 16 and in 1381 to those over 15. This tax was very unpopular and eventually led to the peasants revolt of 1381 and as a result of this it was stopped until the reign of Henry VIII when a

Poll tax on aliens was implemented. A comparison of the tax lists before and after the plague is a strong indication of those who died from the plague.

Taxes on personal wealth, based on income from land, wages and moveable goods was introduced in 1525 through the lay subsidies. Charles I further refined the lay subsidy in 1625 by making it punitive against known Roman Catholics.

Hearth Tax
In 1662 the occupiers of every dwelling were required to pay an annual payment of two shillings for every fire hearth and stove. This tax was abolished in 1668 by William and Mary. The last collection of this tax was the 25th March 1689. Note: Where Parish Registers were damaged after the Civil War the Heath Tax Returns and other taxation records are useful alternative location sources. The number of hearths taxed on a single dwelling is a strong indication of wealth within that household.

Later Stuart Poll Taxes
Charles II imposed graded Poll Taxes in 1660-1668. Everyone over 15 was liable.

Land Tax
Amanda Bevan's book *Tracing Your Ancestors in the Public Record Office* points out that from 1689 to 1830 there are records of land and assessed taxes in local record offices which list names. From 1696 names of proprietors, & occupiers were recorded and taxation sums assessed, payable for one year. This included manors, lands, quarries, annuities and rent charges. Three shillings in the pound on their full yearly value.

Tax on Births, Marriages and Burials
1695 - 1706

Window Tax
1696 A tax which was based on the number of windows in a property and resulted in many windows being bricked up at that time, which can still be seen in properties of that age. Surviving records are usually located in local record offices.

Stamp Duty
Established 1694 and represented charges on legal proceedings, commercial and financial licensing duties imposed on hawkers, pedlars, and shopkeepers. Duties on apprentices levied 1710 - 1811.

Legacy Duty
Legacy duty on personal estates reintroduced 1780 -1796.
Further Legacy Duty Act in 1805 required any real estate directed to be sold to pay legacies.

If you have a rough idea where your ancestors lived tax records are useful as a means of confirming this, and also they can provide an indication of their financial status at that time. Tax records can in general be examined at county record offices. In the case of Surrey these records will be held at PRO Kew.

For a very detailed analysis of taxation through the ages refer to *Family Roots* by Stella Colwell PRO

Death Duty Registers
Death duty registers are very useful in identifying the pre 1858 court in which a will was proved, they may also show relationships not given in the actual will itself.

Tithes
One $1/10^{th}$ of crop harvested was payable to the incumbent of the Parish. Tithe maps dating from the middle of 19th century show apportionment of land in each parish. Records list the names of landowners and occupiers, plot number, name of piece of land, extent of land.

Chapter Eleven

Newspapers, Periodicals and Directories

Newspapers
Copies of newspapers, national and local are held at the British Newspaper Library at Colindale, North London and are available for viewing by the public. Many local record offices hold copies of their own county newspapers on microfilm. Newspapers provide a very useful source of background information which can illuminate the way our ancestors lived and worked in the late 1800s onwards as well as highlighting the significant events which occurred in those times including military service and criminal acts etc. Although domestic newspapers started in 1641 stamp duty taxation in 1712 caused a number to close down and restricted the circulation of others through the cost imposed by this tax. In spite of this the number of newspapers in circulation increased steadily. Eve McLaughlin's booklet *Family History from Newspapers* notes that by 1776, there were 53 newspapers in London.

The duty was abolished in 1861 which resulted in many more newspapers being published. By the late 1800s more detail of ordinary people was included such as births, marriages, deaths and obituaries.

Jeremy Gibson's booklet, *Local Newspapers 1750 - 1920* lists the holdings at the Newspaper Library at Colindale for each county. Under the Surrey section for Reigate and Redhill he notes the following newspapers: Reigate, Redhill, Dorking & Epsom Journal 1863-1902; (Mid-) Surrey Mirror 1879-95, 1901-20+, Surrey Leader 1891-1901 and R & R Gazette 1907-13.

The Surrey & Sussex Newspaper Office at Trinity House, 51 London Road, Reigate also hold back issues of the Surrey Mirror Newspaper, although a number were burnt when the offices located in Ladbroke Road Redhill caught fire back in the early 60s.

Mary Slade of the Holmesdale Natural History Club has indexed selected pages of the 1883 to 1910 Surrey Mirror & General County Advertiser held at Reigate. A copy of the index is held in Redhill Library. Permission to view these Newspapers would need to be obtained by contacting the Surrey Mirror Reigate Office. Access may be granted to serious researchers.

Periodicals

News Magazines such as the Gentleman's Magazine provide a great deal of genealogical information , such as births, marriages deaths and obituaries, although these are likely to apply mainly to the upper classes, tradesmen who served the gentry may also be included. There are many other periodicals that have been produced which provide useful background information for the genealogist. Many early copies are held at the Surrey History Centre, Woking and also at the PRO at Kew. These range from religious group magazines to trade journals. Colin R.Chapman in his booklet. *Using Newspapers and Periodicals* published by the Federation of Family History Societies provides a selected list of periodicals held at the British Library at Colindale which date from 1717 to 1984. The following is a small sample from that list:

Methodist Magazine	1798 - 1932	Baptist Magazine	1809
National School Magazine	1824	Hue & Cry	1828
Poor Law Unions Gazette	1857	Genealogist	1877
Ancestor. Quarterly Review	1906	Genealogical Monthly	1913
Genealogist Magazine (SOG)	1925	Family History	1962

Note: Surrey History Centre, Woking have a run of Gentleman's Magazine 1731 – 1842.

Local Directories

Although the earliest commercial directories were published at the later part of the seventeenth century starting in London they rapidly spread to all areas, these were however primarily intended for business purposes. It was not until the early nineteenth century that private addresses were included, although the early directories usually carried information on the gentry and commercial traders these are valuable to the family historian, as they are probably the quickest way to find out where a person lived at a specific time. By checking each succeeding or preceding year it is possible to established when they first took up residence and when they moved on to another address. Such directories are also useful for tracing the development of the houses in a particular road or street.

Street and commercial directories are held on microfiche at Redhill Library covering Reigate & surrounding districts. These cover the period 1891 to 1954, with some omissions in the series.

Other useful directories are held at the British Library at Colindale, including:
Crockfords Clerical Directory published Annually since 1858
Medical Directory started 1845
Who's Who (First issued 1849)
Who was Who (List the famous who have died)
First issued 1920.
Trade & Commercial Directories
Womans Workers Directory published 1909 by Bale & Danielson
Old Directories of telephone subscribers, BT Archives London.
Universal British Directories. (Published in parts 1790-1798)
Etc.
Note: Redhill Library hold the BT Phone Book on Microfiche for most of the UK. (1991-1995).
Surrey History Centre, Woking hold a number of Crockfords.

Chapter Twelve

Earlier Genealogical Sources

Manorial Records
Generally original manorial documents that have survived are located in the county record offices. The earliest manorial records go back to the time of William the Conqueror and were produced mainly as the means of managing the day to day business of each manor. This included for example such items as the conveyance of land, and court sessions that dealt with major crime and petty offences. There is a manorial document register which is an index giving the location of known existing records, it may be examined at the National Register of Archives, The Royal Commission on Historical Manuscripts, Quality House, Quality Court, Chancery Lane, London, WC2A 1HP.

A useful source book is *Manorial Records* by Patrick Palgrave-Moore, also PRO Readers Guide No.6, *Using Manorial Records* by Mary Ellis, ISBN 1873 162 383. Eve McLaughlin's *Guide to Manorial Records* is also recommended.

The manorial system was active from the time of William the Conqueror until the eighteenth century. Many records have been generated as a result of this system which controlled the lives of those who lived and worked within each manor. These records include such documents as court rolls, surveys & maps, terriers, accounts as well as others. They are invaluable documents which provide evidence of the past and the way of life in villages at specific times. The early medieval manorial records are usually in Latin. English became more common in the sixteenth century.

Traditionally the manor comprised a piece of land upon which may be one or more villages together with a church, dwellings, mainly cottages and houses with tenants and a manor house which was the Lords residence. A significant part of the manor land would be divided up into fields under cultivation, there would also be waste or common land.

Mary Ellis's book, *Using Manorial Records*, PRO readers guide No.6 goes into some detail about the manorial system and points out that the structure of each manor following the conquest consisted of the lord of the manor as supreme head or tenant in chief by grant from the crown with all other land within the manor being held by tenants of the lord. Some were freeholders and held their land by payment of rent and others were not free tenants, they paid rent but were also obliged to provide labour to cultivate the lord's demesne land and to provide other services. The poorest of the manor were the cottars or bordars who held no land and were employed by the lord or freeholders as labourers.

Rules of the manor were established to govern the behaviour of the tenants in relation to one another and in relation to the lord. These rules were enforced through the manor court system which was typically administered by the following offices:

Steward   - Chief officer whose duty was to keep surveys and account rolls
Bailiff   - General Manager, day to day running of the manor.
Reeve   - Forman and overseer of the cultivation of the land.
Hayward - Supervised the maintenance of hedges and fences.

Regular meetings of the court were held to deal with problems which, then developed into formal sessions. (detailed proceedings were recorded in the court rolls)

Manorial Court Rolls
There were generally two main courts sessions held within the manorial system on a regular basis which produced court records namely:

Court Baron:
Court Baron dealt mainly with the registered transfer of copyhold lands, descent of family holdings, death and review of manorial accounts, which included survey assessments of land holdings within the manor and the payment of rentals and fines, the marriage of daughters also required the permission of the lord and incurred a charge.

```
Surveys                         Accounts
custumals  | Detail              Details financial
extents    } income              state of the
rentals    | to Lord             manor
```

A survey of a manor if accompanied by a map is of particular value as it may name each tenant, describe their land acreage and the building on the land.

Court Leet:
Court Leet dealt with day to day matters such as the repair of hedges, maintaining ditches, looking after cattle. Punishment of crime and petty offences against the customs of the Manor. Depending on the seriousness of the offence this could result in anything from a fine to death in the case of a major crime.

Manorial records can provide evidence of the existence of one's ancestors within a manor over several generations. On the death of a father the right of a son to inherit the land held by his father was recognised by the court if proof of right could be established through copyhold documents or known tenure on that land through several generations. To transfer the land from father to son required the payment of a heriot to the lord.

Court Baron part extract of proceeding's record

Extract from Court Baron held at Nutfield Manor in 1738.

Copyright Surrey History Service

Extract of part of Survey carried out for Reigate Manor 1663

A Survey of the Manor of Reigate in the County of Surrey with the Rights & Members and Appurtenances thereof late parcell of the Possessions of William late Lord Viscount of now parcell of the Possessions of his Royal Highness James Duke of Yorke made and taken by me John Fiske in the Month of August 1663 by virtue of an Order of the Right Honorable for the Mannageing the Revenue of his s:d Royall Highness Dated the 20th day of July 1663 —

The Demesnes

The Site of the Castle of Reigate together with the severall parcells of ground within the circuit of the same conteyning 17 acres with the houses thereupon (Viz:t) the Tower consisting of a Hall and parlour and two ... chambers over them and three convenient Lodgeing Rooms in the ... and a Cellar, with other Out Buildings Consisting of a ... a faire roome over it also a Stable a Barne of ... Building a Coach house with a Chamber over it and one other ... adjoyning unto the Barne & one ... Roome and a Chamber over it All which are in reasonable repaire and usefull, there are other Buildings very large which are very much ruined and most of them fallen downe and cannot well be repaired without modifying ... which pmisses are in the Occupation of Michaell Symones Bayliffe the Mannor and is alowed to him towards his Service in executing of that office all the premisses are worth p ann: ... 17 · 0 · 00 20

All that peece of pasture ground called or knowne by the name of the Parkehills lying on the South side of the Towne now in the occupation of the ... of Peterborough from yeare to yeare abutting upon the Roade leading from the towne towards ... on the East upon the highway called Littleton Lane towards the West upon the Lands ... hereafter ... called Grinders coppice towards the South and upon the Meadow called the ... heretofore part of the said parke (and since gained from it by the said Coppices) towards the North which said Parkhills conteyne p est: ... 100 · 0 · 00 9¼ / 40²

60

Example of Rents due to the Lord for Reigate Manor 1700

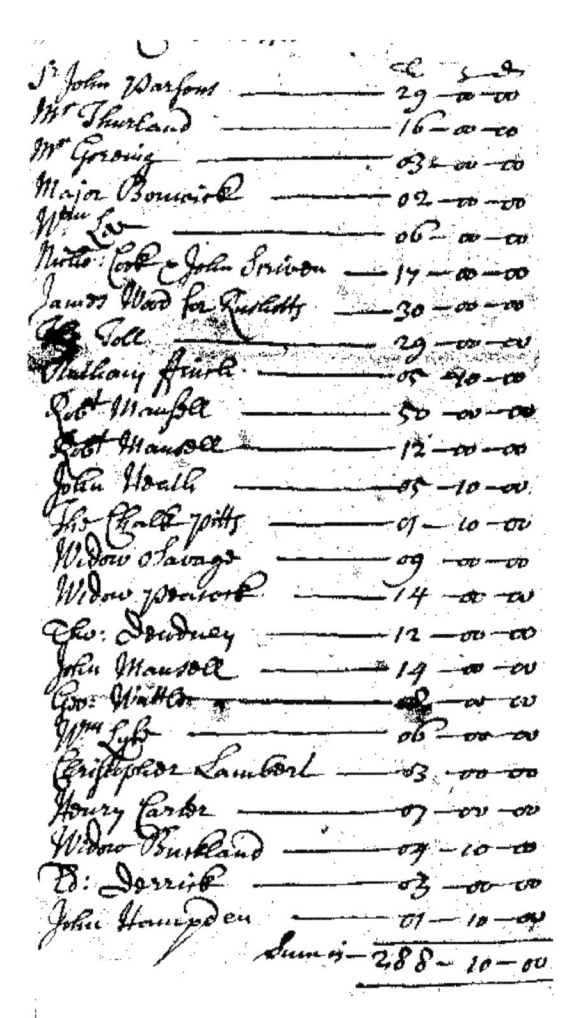

	£	s	d
Sr John Parsons	29	00	00
Mr Thurland	16	00	00
Mr Goring	03	00	00
Major Bonwick	02	00	00
Wm Lu	06	00	00
Nicho Cook & John Scriven	17	00	00
James Wood for Rushetts	30	00	00
Ja Toll	29	00	00
Anthony ffuirla	05	10	00
Rot Mansell	50	00	00
Rot Mansell	12	00	00
John Hoath	05	10	00
Tho Chalk pitts	01	10	00
Widow Savage	09	00	00
Widow Prior	14	00	00
Cho: Dudney	12	00	00
John Mansell	14	00	00
Geo: Winter		00	00
Wm Lyle	06	00	00
Christopher Lambert	03	00	00
Henry Carter	07	00	00
Widow Buckland	07	10	00
D: Derrick	03	00	00
John Hampden	01	10	00
Sum is	288	10	00

Copyright of Surrey History Service

Eve McLaughlin in her book *Manorial Records* clarifies the meaning of a number of words used in manorial documents, for example:

(Franklin)	Free tenant but paid rent and provided service to the Lord
(Heriot)	Originally army equipment taken back; later a charge on transfer of land to heir.
(Virgate)	Piece of land approximately 30 acres, but varied.
(Villeins)	Non free tenant.
(Cottar)	Lesser Serfs with land 4-10 Acres. Cottager who sometimes had smallholding. Had to labour on lords land.
(Bordars)	Living on waste land.
(Quit Rents)	Substitute for services owed to the Lord.
(Burgage)	Land in the towns.
(Custumals)	An inventory of customs & services which Lord was entitled to receive.

The Black Death (1348) decimated the labour on the manors in much of the Country and in the longer term gave the remaining serfs a stronger bargaining position with the lord of the manor, this enabled many of them to secure tenure through copyhold agreements. Hence if your ancestors lived on a manor it is very likely they would have been recorded somewhere in manorial documentation either through land transfers, rentals, surveys or misdemeanours.

A roll film copy of Bletchingley and Nutfield Manorial Court Rolls is available for review at Redhill Library.

Poor Law Records-Before 1834

In current times with the majority of the population either in regular employment, receiving social security benefit or a pension there are very few people who are living in absolute poverty. In earlier times things were very different in this respect. Our ancestors were frequently faced with the problem of survival through difficult times such as lack of employment, sickness, injury or old age. In pre-Reformation England the church through its officers took on the responsibility for looking after the parish poor. An Act of Elizabeth I required the parish officers to feed, clothe and house the poorest of the village and to apprentice pauper children by levying a poor rate on the wealthy and those in employment and using this to provide support to those unable to help themselves. All receipts of money and transactions made were diligently recorded in some detail and hence provides a very important record of village inhabitants and their way of life. Typical poor law documents thus generated included such items as:

Settlement Certificates

To ensure the poor rate was only paid out to those who were recognised as being officially settled in a particular village anyone moving from another village was required to provide evidence of the place of settlement. This took the form of a certificate signed by their original parish officers stating they would accept responsibility for them should they have need to lay claim on the poor relief. Without such a certificate it was unlikely that another village would accept the new arrival. Copies of such settlement certificates were kept in the parish chest.

Settlement Examinations

If there was any doubt as to the right of an individual to claim relief the parish officers would arrange for a settlement examination to take place. Anne Cole in her booklet, *Poor Law Documents before 1830* Notes that settlement examinations are by far the most informative of all poor law records.

Example: (See Quarter Sessions)

Removal Orders
An unsatisfactory settlement examination could well be followed by a removal order causing the offender to be returned to his or her original parish, if they became dependant on poor relief. Removal orders were issued by the courts and are recorded in quarter sessions records. Example: Surrey Quarter Sessions 1663-1666. Copy in Redhill Library.

Apprenticeship Indentures
Many pauper children were apprenticed by the parish, under a master. The apprenticeship was paid for by the parish, unless the parents could afford to pay part of the cost. Two indentures were made out on one piece of paper, one above the other. These were signed by the parish officer, the master and the justices. The paper was cut in half in such a way that the two parts when placed together engaged perfectly. This was to prevent forgery. One copy was kept in the parish chest, the other was held by the master until the completion of the apprenticeship. It would then be handed over to the apprentice. The indenture contains much useful genealogical information, including the apprentice's name, age, trade and the parents' names together with the name of the master. Some apprentices were treated badly by their masters as is evidenced by the following court record:

> *Complaint on behalf of Jeofferey Cooke apprentice to Isaack Benett of Newington, combmaker, who has been beaten and wounded by him that he the said Cooke, has been ten weeks in St Thomas Hospital and is not yet cured. It is preyed he be discharged of his apprenticeship. It is ordered accordingly unless Bennett shows cause to the contrary at the next session.*

Quarter Sessions
It has been previously noted that settlement examinations and removal orders were recorded in quarter session records. Other poor law recorded in quarter sessions includes the issue of bastardy bonds to a father of an illegitimate child, which documents his acceptance to take responsibility

for covering the costs incurred through pregnancy and for bringing up the child. Once the child was born a Maintenance order would be made making it a legal obligation to meet the cost of bringing up the child. If the father absconded a Warrant would be issued to locate him. Once found a summons would be issued to attend the next quarter session.

The poor were frequently in conflict with the law for very petty offences so it is highly probable that our ancestors found themselves being recorded in quarter sessions from time to time for one reason or another. *Anne Cole in her booklet entitled Poor Law Documents before 1830* advises that there are two sources of quarter session records,

files and minute books. She points out that the minute books are far easier to search to locate a particular case before referring to the detailed court files.

Overseers Accounts
These records in general cover the day to day running costs of the parish and detail the provision of clothing, household goods or the payment of bills of the poor.

Churchwardens Accounts
Churchwardens accounts record in general the repairs and maintenance of the church and grounds, the payment of the poor rate by the parishioners etc.

Workhouses
Many of the poor and destitute finished up in workhouses where they eventually died. The workhouse provided shelter and work but was a miserable existence to finish one's days. Even before the Poor Law Amendment Act of 1834 males and females could be kept separate even if they were married. Records of the workhouses can be found in the overseers or churchwardens accounts and also in the quarter session records.

Poor Law Unions

The poor law unions were created by the Poor Law Amendment Act 1834 and replaced the former individual parish system. Under the Act, parishes were combined into Unions which then built one large Union Workhouse paid for by the parishes in the Union and to which they could send their poor. Union Workhouses were administered by a Board of Guardians. For Union Workhouse records look for the minutes, reports etc of the Board of Guardians. By 1841 the inmates of these institutions where built were recorded in the Census returns.

The following publications are recommended reading prior to delving into poor law records:

The Parish Chest by W.E.Tate.	Phillimore
Poor Law Documents before 1834 by Anne Cole	FFHS
Annals of the Poor by Eve McLaughlin	FFHS
Quarter Session Records by JSW Gibson	FFHS

Redhill Library hold copies of:

- Surrey Record Society – *Surrey Quarter Sessions* 1607-1659
    " " " " " " 1661-1663
    " " " " " " 1663-1666

Chapter Thirteen

Local Collections of Genealogical and Historical Material

Redhill Centre for Local & Family History – Redhill Library

Specific resources held at the centre at the time of writing have been cross referenced from each subject chapter. The following however is a summary of the main holdings:

Banns (of intention to marry)
Merstham	1805-1836	Fiche
Nutfield	1754-1812	Fiche

Baptisms
Bletchingley	1538-1906	Fiche	(Most years)
Merstham	1538-1876	Fiche	
Nutfield	1558-1906	Fiche	
Redhill (St John's)	1843-1900	Fiche	
Redhill (St Matthew's)	1843-1900	Fiche	
Reigate (St Mary Magdalene)	1556-1812	Fiche	

Burials
Bletchingley	1813-1910	Fiche
Merstham	1538-1901	Fiche
Nutfield	1558-1876	Fiche
Redhill (St John's)	1843-1875	Fiche
Reigate (St Mary Magdalene)	1556-1812	Fiche

Census

1841 (Fiche)	Bletchingley, Buckland, Gatton, Godstone, Leigh, Merstham, Nutfield Marsh, Redhill, Reigate, South Nutfield.
1851 (Fiche)	Buckland, Chaldon, Chipstead, Gatton, Headley Heath, Kingswood, Redhill, Reigate, Walton on the Hill.
1861 (Film)	Betchworth, Brockham, Buckland, Burstow, Chaldon, Charlwood, Chipstead, Earlswood(Redhill), Gatton, Headley, Horley, Kingswood, Leigh, Meadvale(Redhill), Merstham, Nutfield, Outwood, Redhill, Reigate.
1871 (Film)	Betchworth, Brockham, Buckland, Chaldon, Chipstead, Earlswood(Redhill), Gatton, Headley, Horley, Kingswood, Leigh, Meadvale(Redhill), Merstham, Nutfield, Outwood, Redhill, Reigate.
1881 (Film)	Betchworth, Brockham, Buckland, Caterham, Chaldon, Chipstead, Earlswood(Redhill), Gatton, Kingswood, Nutfield, Redhill, Redhill Institutions, Reigate, Walton on the Hill.
1891 (Fiche)	Betchworth, Bletchingley, Brockham, Buckland, Burstow, Caterham, Chaldon, Charlwood, Chipstead, Gatton, Horley, Kingswood, Leigh, Merstham, Nutfield, Redhill, Reigate, Salfords(Redhill), Walton on the Hill.

The 1881 Census for the UK is available on CD ROM. Copy held by Redhill Centre for Local & Family History.

Directories
Covers complete area locally as per towns/villages above.

Kelly's 1891-1924, 1930, 1931, 1942, 1944, 1951, 1954, 1956, 1959.

Holmesdale 1908, 1914, 1917, 1921, 1923, 1924 – 40, 1942, 1954 1959

Regency 1966 – 68.

Electoral Registers
1875 (Film) Covering whole of East & West Surrey and South London from Abinger – Worplesdon.

1881 (Film) 2 rolls only – area unlisted at present.

IGI International Genealogical Index
1988 Version All English Counties (over 200 Fiche).
Kent, Surrey and Sussex fiche, listed index by fiche no. and surnames.

Land Tax
(Film)	Bletchingley)	
	Buckland)	
	Leigh)	1780 – 1831/2
	Merstham)	
	Nutfield)	
	Reigate	1780 – 1806

Manor Court Rolls

(Film)	Bletchingley	1649 – 1753
	Nutfield	1522 – 1857

Plus few others for North & West Surrey.

Maps (O.S) First and second Edition

These cover Reigate, Redhill and all adjacent parishes.

See complete list in Resource Index file in the Library.

Marriages

(Fiche)	Bletchingley	1538 – 1923
	Merstham	1540 – 1901
	Nutfield	1558 – 1900
	Redhill (St John's)	1848 – 1876
	Redhill (St Matthews)	1867 – 1909
	Reigate (Mary Magdalene)	1556 - 1906

Phone Book (B.T.)

(Fiche) Whole Country – Residential and Business
Years Range: 1991 – 1995

Tithe Apportionments

(Film)	Leigh	1853
	Merstham	1841
	Nutfield	1844
	Reigate	1846

Local History Books
The Redhill Library holds a wide range of local history books, some reproductions of early newspapers, cuttings and a number of photographs of the local area.

Horley Local History Centre
Horley local History Centre is located at Horley Library. Resources available covering Burstow, Charlwood, Horley and Horne, include the 1841 to 1891 Census records on film or microfiche, wills & probate inventories; parish registers from the mid 1500 to early 1900. They also include tithe apportionments and court rolls. Members of this centre have produced a number of local history books which are available for sale at the library. The centre's web site is : www.surreyweb.org.uk/horley-local-history/

North Tandridge Local History Centre
Located in Caterham Valley Library and holds census records, maps photographs and trade directories for the local area

Reigate Priory Museum
Located within the Reigate Priory building adjacent to Reigate Priory School. The Museum presents exhibitions on a wide range of subjects, designed to appeal to both adults and children. The collection includes local history, domestic memorabilia and costume. Opening hours are 2pm to 4.30pm every Wednesday & Saturday. Admission is free (except for school groups)

Holmesdale Natural History Club
This is a private members club, which holds within its archives much useful local historical material, which is of considerable interest to serious local historians. Typically this includes original documents, maps, artefacts and many photographic slides of local places of interest. Contact Mary Slade, Secretary, for further information, at The Museum, 14 Croydon Road Reigate, RH2 OPG.

Croydon Library
An excellent range of local & family history records are available in microfilm and hardback covering Croydon and surrounding parishes.

Minet Library
Although the Minet Library at Lambeth is not exactly local to Reigate it holds a very fine collection of historical material known as the Surrey Collection. This includes a great deal of material covering Reigate and local parishes. Many local roads, properties, farm land, mills etc. are recorded in legal documents, etchings, paintings, photographs and books. An index of material covering the local area is held in Redhill Library. And is well worth checking over if you are researching the local area. You may well find a visit to the Minet Library is worth undertaking. If you plan to visit the Minet Library telephone first and make a booking
Tel: (020) 7926 6076   Closed Wednesdays. Open alternate Saturdays.

East Surrey Family History Society
Microfiche copies of census indexes; poor law, apprenticeship, settlements; monumental inscriptions & parish registers for a number of East Surrey parishes can be purchased for a small charge from this Family History Society. Internet: www.gold.ac.uk/genuki/SRY/esths/publics

If you are interested in delving into your family history it is well worth considering joining a Local Family History Group in your area or in the area you are researching. Your local library can provide contact details. Such a group may well have access to records not available elsewhere. Ideas can also be exchanged with other members. There are benefits to be gained from those members with many years experience. Talks and presentation also give valuable background information, on the location of specific resources and how to access them. Once started there is no turning back, family/local history research is like a detective story, constantly looking for clues followed by the excitement of discovery, which progressively helps to build up a picture of the lives and times of our forebears. It is not surprising that family/local history research frequently become a lifelong hobby.

Select Bibliography

Books & Booklets that have been referred to in the various sections of this publication are listed below. There are many more books available that cover all aspects of genealogical research with new titles being added on a regular basis.

Reigate Its Story Through the Ages	- Wilfred Hooper
Illustrated Handbook to Reigate	- Palgrave
History of Surrey	- Manning & Bray
History of Surrey	- Aubrey
Reigate The Adventures of a Surrey Town	- Taylor
Electoral Registers	- Jeremy Gibson & Colin Rogers
Oxford Guide to Family History	- David Hey
Never Been Here Before (PRO) Readers Guide No 17	- Jane Cox & Stella Colwell
Sources of Roman Catholic & Jewish Genealogy & Family History	- D.J.Steel & Edgar R Samuel
The Family Historian 'Enquire Within Guide'	- F.C.Markwell & Pauline Saul
The Churches of Surrey	- Mervyn Blatch
The History of Merstham School	- John Neal
The History of Redhill Junior Technical School	- Tom Slaughter
St Joseph's Catholic Parish 1855-1955	- T.J.Healy & C.P Spender

Making the most of the IGI — Eve McLaughlin
Where to Look for Wills — J.S.W. Gibson
Wills before 1858 — Eve McLaughlin
Somerset House Wills from 1858 — Eve McLaughlin
Tracing Your Ancestors in the PRO — Amanda Bevan
Family Roots (PRO) — Stella Colwell
Family History from Newspapers — Eve McLaughlin
Local Newspapers (1750-1920) — Jeremy Gibson
Using Newspapers & Periodicals — Colin R. Chapman
Using Manorial Records — Mary Ellis
How to locate & use Manorial Records — Patrick Palgave-Moore
Manorial Records — Eve McLaughlin
The Parish Chest — W.E. Tate
Poor Law Documents before 1834 — Anne Cole
Annals of the Poor — Eve McLaughlin
Quarter Session Records — J.S.W Gibson
Making Sense of the Census — Edward Higgs

Useful Addresses

Redhill Library, Warwick Quadrant, London Road, Redhill, Surrey, RH1 1NN
Tel: (01737) 773204

Horley Local History Centre, Horley Library, Victoria Road, Horley, RH6 7AG
Tel: (01293) 824320

Holmesdale Natural History Club, The Museum, 14 Croydon Road, Reigate, RH2 OPG

Surrey History Centre, 130 Goldsworth Road, Woking, Surrey, GU2 1ND
Tel: (01483) 594594

Public Record Office, Ruskin Avenue, Kew, Richmond, Surrey, TW9 4DU
Tel: (020) 8876 3444; Enquiries (020) 8392 5261

Family Record Centre, 1 Myddelton Street, London, EC1R 1UW
Tel: (020) 8392 5300

Lambeth Archive Department, Minet Library, 52 Knatchbull Road, London, SE5 9QY.
Tel: (020) 7926 6076

Society of Genealogists, 14 Charterhouse Building, Goswell Rd, London, EC1M 7BA.
Tel: (020) 7251 8799

Redhill Centre for Local & Family History, Redhill Library
Tel: (01737) 773204

Dr Williams Library, 14 Gordon Square, London, WC1H OAG
Tel: (020) 7387 3727

The British Library, 96 Euston Road, London, NW1 2DB
Tel: (020) 7412 7626

Guildhall Library, Aldermanbury, London, EC2P 2EJ
Tel: (020) 7332 1863

London Metropolitan Archives, 40 Northampton Road, EC1R OHB
Tel: (020) 7332 3820

LDS Family History Centre, Mormon Chapel, Old Horsham Road Crawley.
Tel: (01293) 516151

Index

Apprenticeship Indentures	77
Arderne Family Brasses,	37
Baptists	29
BishopTranscripts	22
Black Death	74
Burials	26,28
Cemeteries	43,46,47
Census	16-19
Certificates	10-12,20,77
Christchurch, South Nutfield	40,41
Civil Register Index	10,11,13,14,15
Congregationalists	30,46
Copyhold	22,23,24,26,27
Cottars	71
Court Baron	71,72
Court Leet	72,73
Cranston Library	43
Cremation	46,47
Death Duty	66
Directories	69
Education	48
Electoral Registers	20,21
Emmanuel Church, Sidlow	44
Family Record Centre	12,61,63
Freeholders	71
Gatton	49
Grammar School, Reigate	53
Graveyards	34
Hearth Tax	65
Holy Trinity, Redhill	42
Huguenots	32

International Genealogical Index	58,59,60
Jews	32
Jolliffe Family	38
Land Tax	65
Lay Subsidy	64
Legacy Duty	66
Leigh Place	37
Manor Court	71
Manorial Records	70,71
Manorial Survey	72
Marriage Licence	24
Methodists	30,45,68
Monumental Inscriptions	34,36,38
National Register of Archives	70
Newspapers	67,68
Non conformists/records	29,30
Overseer Accounts	79
Parish Registers	22,23,24,26,27
Periodicals	68
Plague	43,65
Poll Tax	64,65
Poor Law	68,77,80
Presbyterians	29,30,46
Probate Records	62,63
Public Record Office Kew	61,63,66,70
Quakers	29,68
Quarter Sessions	29,30,78,79
Recusants	31
Redhill Centre for Local & family History	27,61,69,81-85
Roman Catholic Churches	44
School Records	49-56
Settlement certificates	76

Society of friends	29
St Andrews, Gatton	36,37
St Cross, Chapel	43
St John's Redhill	40
St Katherine, Merstham	38
St Luke, South Park, Reigate	44
St Marjks, Bletchingley	36
St Mark's, Reigate	43
St Mary Magdelene, Reigate	42
St Mary, Bletchingley	35
St Mary, Buckland	34
St Matthew, Redhill	41
St Michael, Betchworth	33
St Peter & St Paul, Nutfield	39
St Philip, Reigate	44
Stamp Duty	66,67,69
Surrey History Centre Records	21,23-26,28,34-36,38 39,41,43,49-56,61 68,73-74
Taxation Records	64,65
Tithes	66
United reformed Church	31
Window Tax	66
Workhouse	79

Other titles in the series by The Redhill Centre for Local & Family History during Year 2000 include:

The History of Redhill Technical School by Tom Slaughter

Reigate & Redhill in Bygone Days by Tony Powell

Royalists, Roundheads and Rogues of Reigate by Brenda Potter

Tudor Times in Reigate by *Tony Powell*